HEART-POWERED SALES

HEART-POWERED SALES

Grow Your Sales Exponentially with Emotional Intelligence and Intuition

ROBIN TREASURE

This book is dedicated to my daughter, Grace.
May you always follow your heart.

"When you are in the Flow of Life,
Doors open easily when you knock,
You know intuitively what your next right step is,
The people you need appear and they offer help gladly,
Coincidences abound.
Opportunity arrives out of the blue.
Life itself is conspiring to help you."

—Tao Te Ching

TABLE OF CONTENTS

INTRODUCTION

"What's your secret?" I've received different forms of this question over the years from colleagues who are all brilliant and ambitious in their own unique ways. After graciously congratulating me for receiving an award or a special spot on a leaderboard, they'd follow up with that question and wait for my answer with openness and readiness to learn. I'd share bits and pieces of what had contributed to my sales growth, but for quite a while, I was hesitant to share the bigger picture, *not* because I wanted to withhold my "secret" from others. In fact, I wanted to shout my secret from the rooftops. I wanted everyone to know it and implement it because in helping one another, our successes and joys are amplified many times over. Success isn't sliced from a finite pie. Instead, one person's success can be shared many times over to inspire others to do the same.

But I didn't share it all because I worried people would think I was crazy. I also doubted that it fit into any legitimate sales methodology. But what I came to realize is that only sharing the "legitimate" bits and pieces without sharing the essential foundation was like giving someone a car without any keys.

Here is the "secret" (the essential foundation): a powerful energy is available to us all, if only we remove the barriers that stand in our way and prevent us from plugging into it. We connect to this powerful energy through the heart. We have a choice. We can either grit our teeth, dig our heels in, and force things to happen . . . or we can surrender, allow for guidance to come from beyond, and focus on service that benefits our customers. Experiencing success in sales and focusing on the highest good of our customers are not mutually exclusive concepts. In fact, the two work in perfect synergy.

Whether you have an official role as a salesperson for your company or whether you represent your own services, I've created the Heart-Powered Sales Method™ specifically for you. I'll teach you how to plug into that powerful energy so you can cultivate your most powerful gifts: emotional intelligence and intuition. The seedlings of both are already inside you, waiting for you to tap into them and help them blossom fully. To do so, you will nurture them through the practical exercises in this book, and you will see how the process involves a simple shift from what you might have been taught until now.

Although I've written this book primarily for women in sales, if you're a man or identify differently, welcome! You're in the right place. The truth is, we all possess the gifts of emotional intelligence and intuition, and we can all benefit from learning to tap into them more. Let's aim to achieve balance and integration in the totality of who we are; this includes all forms of intelligence available to us and all energies of the masculine and feminine, spiritual and physical, doing and non-doing.

Additionally, this material can easily be applied to coaches and healthcare practitioners, and later on, I have a chapter dedicated to you to explain how to apply this method.

In all likelihood, you haven't been given a tailor-made guidebook on how to remain aligned with your core values while achieving your goals for sales growth and even deepening your spiritual connection along the way. Perhaps you picked up this book with no intention of achieving spiritual growth. Maybe you just want to enroll more clients into your coaching programs, or maybe you just want to increase your sales as an outside salesperson. If that's the case—no worries! Whether your end goal is spiritual growth or just more money in your bank account, the path to get you there is exactly the same: through the heart.

Yet, if you do a quick search for the top twenty or thirty books on sales, you will see title after title that includes nearly adversarial words such as persuasion, pitch, sales machine, strategic selling, titans, invincible, sell or be sold, and challenge. In a profession that hinges on communication and relationships, where is the heart?

What you will get from this book

I intend to help you remove the struggle from your sales process, eliminate your fear of being pushy, and overcome the end-of-month quota anxiety. I will show you how to approach your sales from a place of service, purpose, and ease for the mutual benefit of both you and your customers.

After each of the four sections in this book, you will find recommended daily practices to implement what I've shared. Please be sure to download your free HPS Companion Workbook at robintreasure.com/workbook.

By reading this book and consistently applying the practices at the end of each section, you will:

- Learn how to achieve double-digit sales growth without feeling like you're "selling."
- Watch your income grow and enjoy more prosperity.
- Feel like your work is aligned with your heart and soul.
- Make your dreams and desires a reality.
- Become a trusted partner in the eyes of your customers.
- Receive more referrals from customers who respect and value you.
- Experience your work in sales as a springboard for spiritual growth.

My promise to you

Less than a decade ago, sales was the last career I ever thought I'd be in. And yet, now that I'm here and have been blessed to approach this work in a way that comes naturally to me, I know beyond a shadow of a doubt that if I can thrive in this career, so can you. By implementing the Heart-Powered Sales Method™, you will regularly experience win-wins as a norm: your customers will benefit immensely from your service while you enjoy unprecedented growth in your income, sales, confidence, and sense of fulfillment.

After you read this book, you will have a whole new perspective on your work in sales, and you will have a deepened sense of spiritual connection that will positively impact all areas of your life, far beyond your career.

PART 1:

WHAT'S LOVE GOT TO DO WITH IT?

CHAPTER 1: I FOLLOWED MY HEART

On a sunny afternoon as I drove along in Berkeley with the windows rolled down, I smiled to myself in amazement and gratitude. Earlier that day I'd had a Zoom meeting with my regional sales director for a year-end performance review. "Robin," he said, "your total sales for 2020 were $2.8 million, and you grew your territory by twenty-nine percent over 2019." Hearing the official calculation of my numbers for the year helped to make it more real. I was quiet for a moment to let it all sink in. When I had first started with the company almost five years earlier, the annual sales in my territory were $220,000. In less than five years, I'd grown the territory by more than ten times.

As I drove along, later that day, I reflected on the numbers again and mused at how I couldn't have imagined being where I was even a few years earlier. Just then, a Jackson Browne song came on the radio: "Looking out at the road rushing under my wheels; looking back at the years gone by like so many summer fields."

The song immediately took me back to 1981, when I was eight years old. I remembered sailing down the road in my dad's blue Ford pickup truck, with the windows rolled down, my blond braids tossing around in the warm summer breeze. That Jackson Browne song played on the radio, and I smiled back at the wild sunflowers shining their cheerful faces amongst the juniper and pine trees in those mountains of rural New Mexico.

In that summer of 1981, my mom, dad, brother, and I were on our way to a potluck party. My mom held a loaf of freshly baked bread in her lap with a casserole nestled between her feet on the floor of the pickup truck. It was one of the countless parties that took place amongst that broad circle of hippie friends—where the adults hugged and laughed around kegs, while we kids ran around in the *arroyos*, dodging cacti and playing without a care of whether the red dirt would stain our hand-me-down clothes.

After we arrived at the party and I hugged the people I knew, I remember becoming aware of a powerful feeling in my heart. This was both a capability as well as a feeling of joy, light, and love that allowed me to be attuned to other people's emotional states and needs. I was too young to question it or analyze where it came from. I was simply aware of this presence and how people seemed to be drawn to it. I knew they weren't responding to me. Instead, they were responding to the presence that was coming through me, even if others were not aware of the distinction. All I had to do was be open to this presence, and it was like a switch had suddenly turned on in my heart. From there, I could feel what other people felt, and I could shine a light that would comfort and uplift those who needed it. For those who were joyful, I reflected their joy back to them.

About an hour into that party, most of the adults were outside playing volleyball, while I was inside the house with a handful of other kids. One of them was a three-year-old boy named Aaryn. He had just used his potty and came out to announce that he had gone number two, but the toilet paper had run out. Glancing over at the dining table where an adult had left their rolling papers after rolling several joints, Aaryn's face lit up. He confidently grabbed the pack of rolling paper, pulled out several sheets, and wiped his bottom with a satisfied grin on his face.

We, kids, laughed at the absurd genius of Aaryn's idea. Just then, Aaryn's mom walked in the door, and we relayed the story to her. As she joined in our laughter, I remember how poignantly I felt the mix of thoughts and emotions in that room: the way Aaryn squirmed with embarrassment at being the center of attention, the other kids' joy in laughing all together, the spark of perplexed curiosity that Aaryn's mom felt along with the amused smile on her face, my own aware-ness of how we children were too young to be so familiar with things like beer kegs and rolling papers, and the way the come-dy provided a comfy layer of relief from the inappropriateness of the situation. Yet above all else, I had that loving presence in my heart that told me everything was okay, no matter what. All that really mattered was the love that abounded.

Even though that party was no different from the many other parties that had come before and after, it was significant because I had become aware of being connected to a powerful, loving presence that was much greater than myself. From that age, that presence never left me—though it waxed and waned and morphed many times over. During a few periods in my life, I unconsciously shut myself off to it, resulting in unnecessary heartache and grief. Thankfully, those darker periods were brief, and in a matter of time, I opened back up to that loving presence. As a result, I was guided by my heart in every major decision I ever made, and I remained attuned to the feelings and desires of other people. This served as an enormous gift that eventually led me to a career in sales—after many twists and turns in a path that seemingly led in completely different directions.

Loving consciousness

I've since realized that this loving presence is with everyone, always. Some refer to this presence as God or Universe. I like to refer to it as loving consciousness because it is more universally accessible and is directly connected to the heart. We're all able to feel into our heart as an energy center that emits and receives love. This can be love for or from a person, animal, or nature. It can be the love that we feel for and from a higher power or consciousness that gives us joy, light, and guidance.

Loving consciousness, the seat of creation, holds the potential for unlimited possibilities to become reality. It is continually guiding us and responding to our thoughts, feelings, and desires. The result is an interconnected dance between us and the experiences, synchronicities, vibrations, people, thoughts, and feelings that we all experience day in and day out. When you join forces with loving consciousness, it's like hopping onto a raft that glides down a river, bringing you toward more joy and prosperity than you could have ever imagined.

This energy of love is available to us all. The only difference is that some people can access it more readily than others. Some are prevented from accessing it because of the layers of worry, insecurity, fear, trauma, and hardship that they accumulate over time. As Joe Dispenza writes in his book *Breaking the Habit of Being Yourself*, "Our purpose is to remove the masks and the facades that block the flow of this divine intelligence and to express this greater mind through us."

Since I was raised within a culture of people who valued love and happiness above wealth and societal expectations, I could more readily remove my masks and facades to access my own heart.

In fact, my parents had become silent icons of the flower child, peace-and-love generation when a candid shot of them bathing in a pond at Woodstock later appeared on the inside cover of the Woodstock album. Soon after that historic concert, they moved from the East Coast to New Mexico and built the log cabin on a mountaintop where my little brother and I were raised. My dad worked so hard building custom homes for other people in Santa Fe that our own cabin never had the "finer details," like finished plaster between the logs. For a few years, we didn't even have running water, so we bathed in a round aluminum tub with water that my mom heated on our wood-burning stove.

I knew I was fortunate to be growing up in a culture of people who valued freedom, love, and happiness, but it seemed that unconsciously my parents and their friends believed that happiness and wealth were somehow mutually exclusive. So I resolved that when I grew up, I would create a life that allowed for wealth and love and happiness. But the question was, how would I go about doing that? If I aimed for a high-paying job in sales, for example, wouldn't that mean I was selling out? Above all, wouldn't I be automatically "disqualified" from a career in sales when my nature and nurture were all about peace and love? I didn't even know how I would afford a college education, much less move away from the mountaintop where I was raised.

So how exactly does a slightly shy hippie child who grew up in a log cabin go from that world to growing a sales territory in dietary supplements worth $2.8 million? Was it a straight path in the pursuit of wealth? Certainly not. It was a zigzag path with scholarships, hard work, seemingly unrelated career choices, detours living abroad, and enormous amounts of good fortune. Yet the overarching thread of navigation can be traced clearly, every step along the way: I followed my heart.

The gift that I received as a child is what it means to be

heart-powered: connecting to loving consciousness through the heart and being attuned to the emotional state of others. Being heart-powered is the reason for my success in sales, and I promise it will do the same for you. As you will see, the Heart-Powered Sales Method™ entails not only the heart but also equal amounts of dedication, strategy, follow-up, and skill. I will share every step of this method with you in these pages.

How I found sales (or how sales found me)

Sales is a second career for me, and in some ways, it was the last career I thought I'd ever have. First I worked as an Italian translator, both in Italy and the US. When people would ask me why I became an Italian translator, they'd assume I had Italian heritage. "No Italian heritage," I'd reply. "I just fell in love with the language when I started studying Italian my freshman year of college." Essentially, I followed my heart.

After completing a master's degree in Italian translation, I moved to Rome with no job, a mere thousand in savings, five suitcases, and one friend-of-a-friend to call on when I got there. Other than that, I had no plan. Not only did it work out but I thrived in Rome for four years. I made a good living translating screenplays and subtitles in the film industry and doing admin work in the wine industry. I formed lifelong friendships, enjoyed weekend jaunts to the Tuscan countryside, and had unforgettable dinners overlooking night-lit Roman ruins. When I eventually moved back to the US, that invaluable experience enabled me to secure a coveted position at the Italian Cultural Institute.

If I had followed logic, I would've never had those experiences in Italy. If I'd allowed fear to hold me back, I would've pursued a much safer, far less exciting path. Instead, I did what had come naturally to me since childhood: I followed my heart. Through my heart, I was guided by loving consciousness to realize my potential and to push the boundaries of what was possible. With loving consciousness by my side, I continuously met kind, helpful people and found serendipitous opportunities for adventure, friendships, and prosperity.

Toward the end of my translation career, that same plucky desire in my heart compelled me to leave the Italian world and become a health coach. I had been passionate about health and nutrition for many years, and I felt called to help people live healthier lives. After my training and launching my business, I learned that any kind of solo practice is a boot camp training in sales! Not only does your livelihood depend on enrolling clients but the sales process never ends because each session involves "selling" the clients on the lifestyle changes that are necessary for them to feel better.

In the three years that I had my solo health coaching practice, I was unwittingly being groomed for a career in sales. My knowledge of health and nutrition, combined with what I learned about sales, served as the perfect springboard that enabled me to say yes when I heard of an outside sales position at a supplement company that I knew and loved.

Mind you, when a friend in the industry first told me

about the open position, my first instinct was to blurt out, "But I'm no salesperson!" What enabled me to embrace the opportunity was the way my friend reframed the sales role as being fundamentally about service.

After I was hired and got out into the field, I always kept this perspective of service in mind. By creating and following the Heart-Powered Sales Method™ that I went on to develop, I achieved annual growth rates in my territory of 30 to 60 percent each year for five years—without having had any prior experience as an outside salesperson.

The loving consciousness that had guided me in each previous step in my life was now my veritable "sales assistant" in my role as a salesperson. Each day, as loving consciousness guided me, I honed the best questions to ask my customers, the most effective strategies to grow my territory, the surest way to exceed my quotas, and the clearest path to serving my customers in a way that would prompt them to exclaim again and again, "You're the best rep ever!" Receiving kudos was, of course, gratifying, but more than anything, it was a confirmation that following my heart was the way to create the best outcome for all involved. Not only was I enjoying the opportunity to serve through sales and bringing value to my customers but I was also making more money than I ever imagined possible.

Now, I will teach you how to connect to loving consciousness, along with the practical approach and techniques I've used, so you can enjoy the unlimited success that is waiting for you at this very moment.

CHAPTER 2: THE SECRET TO YOUR SUCCESS

In sales, you have the freedom to make many decisions throughout your day: which customers you will call on, where the new leads are, what to discuss during your sales meetings, how to structure your days, and more. Not only can each decision dramatically influence the outcome of each day but each and every thought that you think contains an energetic quality that will attract more of that same energetic quality into your life. If you spend all day thinking about how frustrated and overwhelmed you are, you will suddenly find yourself with more frustrating and overwhelming circumstances to deal with. If you think of all the things you're grateful for throughout the day, you will experience even more good fortune to be grateful for. Where your attention goes, energy flows.

Deepening your spirituality

By approaching sales using the method in this book, you can enjoy more professional success and achieve exponentially more personal growth, happiness, and spiritual connection. Just like I realized that sales was a central component of my health coaching practice (not just an inconvenient task akin to admin work), I encourage you to think of sales as the core platform for your spiritual development (rather than thinking of sales as a way to make a living so you can become more spiritual in your off-hours).

People tend to approach their spirituality as something separate from their professional life—like something that happens only on the meditation pillow or out in nature. Many people may feel the most spiritually "on" when they are praying or reflecting on their connection to divinity, in whatever form they envision divinity to be. Meditation and prayer can certainly be times when we're most connected, and it's important to engage in some form of meditation or prayer every day. Yet each and every moment of our lives offers an opportunity for spiritual growth, even in sales—or dare I say, especially in sales.

When you're meditating or praying, the only challenge is the "noise" of your thoughts or fears (those alone can be a lot to overcome). Yet the rubber hits the road when you are out in the world, interacting with customers and clients and having to confront the objections and obstacles they present to you. The thoughts and fears you experience in those moments will constantly attempt to pull you out of your heart and up into your head. Your work is to keep dropping back into your heart, and as you keep doing so, you will flex your spiritual "muscles" to help you grow stronger and stronger.

Let's dive deeper into how a difference in mindset can shape you and your sales process, and then let's look at how to access this mindset and heart-centered state in order to drive greater success in your sales.

A difference in mindset

First, allow me to present two contrasting scenarios. See which of these two you might recognize from a day in your own sales career. (Spoiler alert: the external circumstances in both scenarios are exactly the same. The only difference between scenario 1 and scenario 2 is the way you approach it.)

Scenario 1: You're getting ready to head to a scheduled meeting with your customer, Dr. Smith, to present him with a new product that you hope will be of interest. Before you head out the door, you look at your sales dashboard. It's the middle of the month and you've been inching your way toward your monthly quota, but it still looks like a steep climb to the summit. Your mind races as you wonder whether you can meet your quota this month and whether this next meeting with Dr. Smith will result in a sale.

You arrive at Dr. Smith's office, and as soon as you lay eyes on him, you can see he's in a hurry and has very little time for you, even though the meeting was on his calendar. "I won't

take much of your time today, Dr. Smith," you say quickly.
"I just wanted to let you know about this new formula that
we have to support blood sugar balance. This product is novel
because it contains this key ingredient that has been shown to
balance blood sugar very effectively."

"Ah. I'm actually already using a product for blood sugar
that seems to be working well for my patients," he says, and
then adds that the product is made by your competitor. As
he speaks, your thoughts race and the blood drains from your
face. You realize you should have asked him more questions,
but your nerves had gotten the best of you. Plus, he was clearly
in a hurry, so you didn't want to impose or take too much of
his time.

"Oh, okay," you stammer. "In that case, I understand, but
I'll go ahead and leave you this brochure just in case you want
to review it."

"Yes, please do!" he replies quickly but politely as a cue
that the meeting has ended, so he can get on with his day.

You leave the office with a queasy feeling in your gut and
with your shoulders in knots. As you drive to your next meeting, ahead of schedule, you pass by an office that could be a
good lead, but you decide not to stop in because you can't
face the rejection today. The rest of the day proceeds similarly
without any sales. "Oh well"—you sigh— "tomorrow is a new
day."

Scenario 2: You're getting ready to head to a scheduled
meeting with your customer, Dr. Smith, to discover whether
a new product will suit him in his practice. You've taken a few

minutes to envision the day unfolding smoothly, and you've reviewed your goals and business plan. Then you look at your sales dashboard. It's the middle of the month and you've been inching your way toward your monthly quota, but it still looks like a steep climb to the summit. You remind yourself to remain committed to the actions outlined in your business plan and to check in with your intuition regularly. Above all, you remember that you are not alone, as loving consciousness is always with you, whether you are listening or not.

You arrive at Dr. Smith's office, and as soon as you lay eyes on him, you can see he's in a hurry and has very little time for you, even though the meeting was on his calendar. After you greet one another, you say, "Dr. Smith, I can see you're extremely busy today, so we can keep today's meeting very brief." You can see him relax a bit. "We have a new product for blood sugar support, but since that will take a little time to review, let's save that for next time." You see him relax a bit more, then you continue. "And to help me prepare for the next meeting, can I ask you—what are you currently using for blood sugar support in your patients?" He mentions a competitor's product. You remain unattached to whether you make a sale at that moment, and instead, you are committed to supporting the best solution for your customer, even if that means it isn't your product. "Okay, thank you for letting me know. Would it be okay if we explore our newest options for blood sugar support in our next meeting to make sure you have the best options for your patients?" He nods, and you schedule your next meeting with him.

You exit his office feeling grateful for the information he shared because it will allow you to study up on the product he currently uses. You also plan to ask him follow-up questions on what he likes about that product and to find out what else might be important to him. You didn't make a sale, but instead, you feel gratitude for the information you gathered in that brief meeting and for the opportunity it could bring in the future. Feeling the gratitude keeps you anchored in your heart.

As you drive to your next meeting, ahead of schedule, you pass by an office that could be a good lead. You're relaxed and able to notice a warming sensation in your gut. "You should stop into that office," your gut tells you.

It's a chiropractic office that works with patients suffering from sports injuries. You instinctively know that one formula, in particular, is going to suit this office perfectly. You walk in smiling, head held high, excited about how perfectly this product suits this practice.

Just in that moment, the chiropractor steps out of his office and into the front desk area. You're able to address both him and the front desk person by quickly introducing yourself and concisely describing the benefits of the one specific product you have in mind for them.

The chiropractor says, "Oh wow. Just last week I heard about your company, and I was thinking of reaching out. I'm glad you stopped in. I have a patient in a few minutes, but could you come back in an hour?" You return in one hour, engage in a quick but effective meeting to help identify the products that will best serve him, then he places a nice opening order.

You leave that office with a great awareness of the divine orchestration involved in having caught the chiropractor at just the right moment by heeding your gut feeling. The experience presents you with even more evidence of the unlimited possibilities that exist for meeting your goals and exceeding your quota for the month.

You proceed to have a couple more meetings that day. You feel great joy, wonder, and gratitude for the way the day unfolded, knowing that it was your trust and connection to loving consciousness that allowed those positive events to occur.

What makes the difference

In the initial setup, there was very little difference between scenario 1 and scenario 2. The day started with your sales dashboard showing the same amount in your sales quota, and Dr. Smith was in exactly the same rushed state in both scenarios. The key difference was the positive energy you had going into the meeting with Dr. Smith. Your frame of mind and your connection to, or disconnection from, loving consciousness is what determines the cascade of events that follow. In both scenarios, it was unlikely that Dr. Smith would place an order that very same day. But responding to Dr. Smith with emotional intelligence while remaining connected to loving consciousness (rather than reacting to Dr. Smith and trying to force a sale out of scarcity or fear) led to a dramatically different outcome as the day unfolded.

Of course, it is critical to adopt the most effective strategies for growing your business and engaging with your customers. Yet even if you are equipped with the best strategies and scripts in the world, can you see how your thoughts and energy will have a direct impact on how effective they are?

Accessing energy, abundance, ease, and joy

A whole other dimension to your success in sales hasn't been given the attention it deserves: in this very moment, you have access to an energy of abundance, ease, and joy that will guide you in your day-to-day work, so you can achieve the success you desire without burning out, selling out, or being "salesy." This energy of abundance, ease, and joy is what I refer to as loving consciousness. Once you align with loving consciousness as the first step in your path to sales success, everything else will unfold naturally, and the techniques and strategies you implement will be effective because you are in your heart.

It's like a dream I once had: I was walking through the desert, pulling a camel who dragged reluctantly behind me. That camel was miserable and so was I, toiling across the sand, in the heat. Then it occurred to me that the camel could carry me. I climbed up onto the camel, and suddenly, we were soaring through the desert—almost flying. Not only did I feel so happy and relieved but the camel was also joyful and delighted in being able to carry me. As we soared through the desert, we were overjoyed by the forward motion and momentum that we shared.

Like the camel, the energy of loving consciousness is here to carry you. It wants to help you glide toward whatever it is that you desire. It wants to be utilized by you, as soon as you connect to it.

In her book *Big Magic*, Elizabeth Gilbert writes about the divine inspiration that can come to your assistance in your creative work. Her beautiful description, which I will quote here, could just as easily be applied to your work in sales:

Sometimes, when I'm in the midst of writing, I feel like I am suddenly walking on one of the moving sidewalks that you find in a big airport terminal; I still have a long slog to my gate, and my baggage is still heavy, but I can feel myself being gently propelled by some exterior force. Something is carrying me along—something powerful and generous—and that something is decidedly not me.

You may know this feeling. It's the feeling you get when you've made something wonderful, or done something wonderful, and when you look back at it later, all you can say is: "I don't even know where that came from."

You can't repeat it. You can't explain it. But if felt as if you were being guided.

I only rarely experience this feeling, but it's the most magnificent sensation imaginable when it arrives. I don't think you can find a more perfect happiness than in this state, except perhaps falling in love. In ancient Greek, the word for the highest degree of human happiness is eudaimonia, which basically means "well-daemoned"—that is, nicely taken care of by some external divine creative spirit guide. (Modern commentators, perhaps uncomfortable with this sense of divine mystery, simply call it "flow" or "being in the zone.")

It's this very energy that will guide you and make your work in sales so much more productive and meaningful. As Elizabeth Gilbert notes, you still have to walk to your gate and carry your heavy luggage (i.e., you still have to do the work—which we will cover in detail later in this book), but a benevolent force will make your work much more fruitful and easeful along the way.

A shift in perspective

Sales is fundamentally about service. It is about serving the needs of your client and offering them the best solution to meet those needs. Even more so, it is about serving your client as a whole person, not just a client with problems to be addressed. This means understanding that emotions are the driving force behind all decisions and sales engagements. For this reason, one of your main objectives must be to interact with your clients with heart-centered emotional intelligence, so your clients feel listened to and understood. Even though you have your own needs and desires, you must set your personal motivations and fears aside to best serve your client. In doing so, you will actually experience more benefits in the long run.

It's important to qualify that the service involved in sales is an energetic exchange—not a one-way act of charity. You are dedicating time and energy to helping them identify what they need, and the best solutions to meet those needs. In turn, the client has to meet you halfway by committing to having honest discussions, providing further information when needed, and investing in your product or service if it's the right fit for them. The end result is a win-win for all.

For this reason, you can know and expect that your efforts will be rewarded, but in your day-to-day work, you must approach each meeting without attachment to the outcome. When you release attachment and when you drop all thoughts of fear or scarcity, you can then take a heart-centered approach, where energy is free to circulate between you and your collective client base. This is what allows for the energetic exchange that naturally arises within a healthy sales process.

But how can you release attachment when your income is connected to the outcome? It's hard, I know! But being heart-powered does not mean being passive. Being heart-powered does not mean you will never ask for the sale. It means you remain committed to the best outcome for your client. If you know your client will benefit from utilizing your product or service, you will have to transcend your own fears and take a stand for your client by leading them to the sale. If instead your client is better served by a competitor's product that they are already using, you must remain unattached to the sale but loyal to the relationship. This may mean asking for a referral from them instead or pursuing other channels of business with the client if you have other offerings to suit them.

This is why sales is the best platform for your own spiritual growth: your work is to remain in your heart, stay committed to serving your client, and overcome your own fears and theirs (sales presents lots of opportunities to practice this!). All the while, you will do the work, follow your business plan, know your numbers, and aim to exceed your quotas. Yet by remaining in your heart, you will show up in a way that will allow you to achieve more than you ever thought possible.

Even after reading this last paragraph, are you afraid that by making sales a spiritual practice, you will become an altruistic softie who never makes a sale and is broke by the end of the month? Let me assure you that the result will be quite the opposite. You will never be asked to forget your sales quotas or abandon your desire for prosperity. Instead, your quotas and desires will be alive and well (but on the sidelines) while you gently shift into being connected to loving consciousness. In doing so, you will actually find yourself on the fast track to achieving your goals, helping more customers, and making more money. You will experience more prosperity because of (not in spite of) being in your heart. The only trick is releasing your attachment to the outcome.

Loving consciousness is waiting to become your "sales assistant" so it can help you meet your business goals. So now let's look at exactly how you can access this powerful force.

CHAPTER 3: THE WAY TO THE HEART

You may have an unconscious belief that you have to hustle in order to experience growth and success. You've probably seen that the go-getters are the ones who rise to the top. Of course, your work requires good measures of dedication and follow-through. But the reality is, if you hustle while resisting or ignoring the energy of loving consciousness, you will have to work twice as hard, and you will only enjoy half the results. All the while, you will be relying on your mind and grit, while the vast resources of your heart and intuition remain untapped. Why wouldn't you lean in to these gifts?

Even if you're naturally inclined to approach life from a heart-centered place, you've most likely been taught to prioritize strategy and logic. If a gut feeling whispers something to you that defies reason, you may wind up feeling confused and overwhelmed, or your logical brain may override your gut. Let's look at how to create coherence between your head and heart so your thoughts and emotions are fully aligned. To achieve this, you must start by giving yourself full permission to be in your heart. There's no need to fear that you will become irrational or illogical. You will always have reason when you need it.

The way to the heart is not a laborious process. It doesn't require any extra time or work. All it requires is a gentle shift in your attention and energy, and you can get there quite quickly. Once you've dropped into your heart, you'll have a positive feedback loop where you feel more joy, connection, positive influence, and impact. Indeed, you will be heart-powered.

To become heart-powered, first surrender

The key to connecting to your heart is to surrender. We expend so much energy in our thoughts and emotions by resisting the flow of life, reasoning our way through every challenge, and muscling our way through every obstacle. In essence, we spend a lot of energy resisting what is. We resist the way our numbers look. We resist feeling tired and needing more rest. We resist the fact that we didn't make a sale in the last meeting, so we wind up feeling more frustrated. In essence, many of us spend a good part of our lives going upstream, resisting what is, and we end up burning out as a result.

So what does it really mean to surrender? Does it mean giving up? No! Surrendering is one of the most powerful actions you can take. Surrendering means you stop wasting your mental and emotional energy on resistance, and instead, you sync up your energy with the forces of loving consciousness. Surrendering means you see things as they are, without trying to change things or wishing you could change them. Then you ask loving consciousness, "What would you have me do? Please show me the way." Immediately, you will become empowered with wisdom and guidance from beyond yourself. From there, things will unfold more naturally.

When I interviewed Camila Arri-Nudo, independent area director for Cutco Closing Gifts, about the importance of "actively surrendering," she pointed to a tattoo on her arm of a person pulling a boat. "This is a reminder that you have to pull life toward you, but at the same time, you just have to ride the waves . . . It gives me a lot of peace to know that. To feel that the higher power and I are working together."

Camila described how active surrender enables her to find success more easily. While noting the importance of staying in action, she also says, "It doesn't have to be hard to be worth it." She recalled that in one of her biggest sales months ever, she was in this state of active surrender. She had five sales meetings in a row that all flowed naturally, where she didn't have to ask for the sale, and all five customers placed an order of their own initiative.

When you surrender, you still have goals and desires for specific outcomes in your life, but now you remove the mental and emotional attachment that says things have to be a certain way.

When you find yourself frustrated or demoralized in a certain situation, you might feel like throwing a tantrum. We've all been there. We all have an inner child that is stubborn and behaves like a brat when they don't get what they want. In fact, use the acronym BRAT for steps on how to surrender:

- Breathe and come back to the present moment
- Release attachment to a certain outcome
- Ask for help and guidance from loving consciousness
- Trust that things will work out exactly as they are meant to

You are not alone. Loving consciousness wants to help you. When you surrender and ask for guidance, the help will come. Although things may turn out differently from what you expected, it's always for the best.

Imagine you're hiking on an unfamiliar trail in the mountains, and it's twilight so you can hardly see the path. A friend next to you offers their help because they know the path well, but you decline. You think you know best. You try to see where the path is leading ahead, but you stumble on rocks you hadn't seen right beneath you. Now you tense up because you're afraid of falling, but because you're tense, you're more likely to fall and hurt yourself. "Just let me help you," your friend says again. And so you surrender. You take a deep breath and release attachment to knowing where the path leads. You ask your friend for help, and you trust that your friend will lead you the right way. As you hook arms with your friend, your body relaxes, making you more able to sense the rocks beneath your feet. You trust your friend, and now you're moving along the path with greater ease.

This is what it means to surrender and join forces with loving consciousness. When you surrender, you drop out of your head, where your logical mind says things have to proceed in a certain way. Far from being a passive or meek action, surrendering is an intentional, empowered choice that enables you to 10X your influence and efficacy in your field, because you are getting out of your way.

Next, activate your heart center

After you surrender, bring your awareness to the physical area of your heart center. Then activate your heart center by focusing on the love and gratitude that you feel for any person, pet, or thing. Feel into the tenderness of your heart. Allow the love that you feel to radiate outward. Notice the powerful stillness within your heart. Listen to the unwavering voice of what you know to be true, deep within your heart. Here, centered in this energy, you are heart-powered, which means you are:

- Relaxing and loosening your mental grip on life
- Letting go of thoughts of fear and scarcity
- Becoming vulnerable, which allows for connection with others
- Feeling the powerful, energizing force of love
- Syncing up with loving consciousness
- Trusting that you will receive the guidance you need

By bringing awareness to your heart center, you will be attuned to the signs that signal you're on the right track. Essentially, you can follow the breadcrumbs, like Hansel and Gretel did. Be on the lookout for signs on your path—both positive and negative—that help guide you along the way. From there, you keep following the positive signs that reinforce the decisions you make. For example, if you walk into a client's office without a scheduled meeting and they say, "Wow, I was just going to send you an email. Perfect timing!" This is a direct affirmation that you're on the right track.

An example of a negative sign would be showing up for a meeting at the final stages of closing a deal and having the client rudely inform you that they decided to go in a different direction. Do your due diligence and ask them what prompted the change of mind, but if you sense a loss of integrity and respect in the relationship, let it go. Better opportunities await you as soon as you release this one.

You may have heard of the story recited by mindfulness master Jon Kabat-Zinn about how a farmer in India found a way to catch monkeys that were destroying his crops. He cut a small hole in a coconut, just big enough for a monkey to fit its hand inside. The farmer then put a banana inside the coconut and tied it to a tree. The monkey came up, smelled the banana, and stuck its hand into the coconut to get the banana. When the monkey tried to pull its hand out, it was unable to because its hand was clenching the banana so it wouldn't fit back through the small hole. And because the monkey refused to let go of the banana, it was caught by the farmer. If only the monkey had let go, it would be free. There are plenty more bananas (opportunities) to be had if only you can let go of attachment.

Activating your heart center and surrendering will help you let go of the sales that don't matter, so you can focus on the ones that do. Please note, that when I say surrender, I don't mean you have to give up on achieving what you desire. Not at all. Your desires are the critical starting point—the impetus—for your actions. Yet it's the attachment to a particular outcome that will make you rigid and resistant to loving consciousness. Attachment will keep you in your logical mind, which says that a certain sequence of events must happen. You may think you know what will bring you happiness and joy, but if you surrender and join forces with loving consciousness, it will help you find that happiness and joy tenfold, in ways you may not have thought possible.

Using coherence to get what you want

Even though I emphasize the importance of dropping down into your heart, what happens in your head is equally important. Every thought that you think has the power to influence your internal and external world. This means that your thoughts will directly impact your feelings, experiences, loved ones, and clients. The key is to establish coherence between your head and heart, so you're fully aligned in who you are and fully tapped into loving consciousness.

Author Joe Dispenza, one of the leading experts on how to integrate your head and heart, writes extensively on neuroscience, quantum physics, brain chemistry, emotion, and meditation. In his book *Breaking the Habit of Being Yourself*, he shows exactly how and why your thoughts become your reality. He also shows how emotions, which are physically expressed as chemicals in the body, tend to reinforce old thoughts. These old thoughts manifest physically and reinforce the undesirable patterns in our lives.

Imagine you've missed your sales quota for several months in a row. If your thoughts create your reality, why doesn't it work to simply "think positive" and envision yourself exceeding your sales quota next month? Emotion is the answer. If you're feeling fearful and frustrated over having missed your sales quota in the last few months, those emotions translate into feelings that get stored in your body as actual chemicals. These chemicals then drag your thoughts away from "thinking positive" back into the old, familiar thoughts of "I missed my sales quota the last couple of months."

What's the solution? Choose your thoughts carefully and combine them with an elevated feeling such as love, joy, and gratitude in order to create coherence.

Yes, at each and every moment, you have the ability to choose your thoughts. Which thoughts will you choose: thoughts of how you missed sales quota last month or thoughts of how you will exceed your sales quota next month? Choose the latter. Then allow yourself to feel the joy of exceeding your quota—now! Feel it as if it has already happened. Don't wait for the evidence of exceeding your quota to feel your joy. Feel the joy in your heart now and envision the exceeded quota now. This will generate the feel-good body chemicals that will inform the brain that a new reality is possible.

As Joe Dispenza writes:

When you have thoughtfully rehearsed a future reality until your brain has physically changed to look like it has had the experience, and you have emotionally embraced a new intention so many times that your body is altered to reflect that it has had the experience, hang on . . . because this is the moment the event finds you! And it will arrive in a way that you least expect, which leaves no doubt that it came from your relationship to a greater consciousness—so that it inspires you to do it again and again.

Notice the integration of mind, heart, body, and intuition in this description. These different forms of intelligence are all aspects of loving consciousness. By integrating these aspects of ourselves, the resulting coherence allows us to manifest more than we ever thought possible. Let's look at those different forms of intelligence now.

CHAPTER 4: UNTAPPED FORMS OF INTELLIGENCE

It would be senseless to argue that when considering the head and the heart in business, you should only go with the heart. Both the head and the heart matter. But we overvalue our logical minds and underutilize the vast amounts of power, influence, and information that derive from outside the logical mind. When we can integrate all forms of intelligence available to us, then the magic happens.

The full scope of our intelligence can be broken down into four categories, as described by author and healthcare practitioner Lissa Rankin, MD. She defines these four categories as:

- Emotional Intelligence (tracking feelings, following your heart, riding the waves of emotions)
- Somatic Intelligence (body wisdom, gut instincts, physical symptoms/sensation)

- Intuitive Intelligence (intuition, divine intelligence, spiritual insights, visionary intelligence, dreaming)
- Mental Intelligence (logic, rational thought, linguistic ability)

Everyone is "equipped" with all four forms of intelligence, although different people will be stronger in different areas. We live in a world where mental acumen is the most prized form of intelligence (think of our focus on strategy, expertise, and knowledge). Emotional intelligence is also gaining more recognition for its impact on business. Yet every single one of these forms of intelligence (including somatic and intuitive) will contribute to your success in sales in different ways.

The benefits of drawing from all forms of

intelligence

Can you imagine how much more impactful you could be if you were able to fully access each form of intelligence when you needed it most? Can you imagine how much more information and guidance would be available to you each day if you were able to quickly draw upon your somatic and intuitive intelligence when you needed it most? By flexing your emotional intelligence, can you imagine how much less fear you would feel about being perceived as pushy or salesy when meeting with a customer? Most importantly, by knowing how interconnected each form of intelligence is with loving consciousness, consider how much more confident you would feel in each decision you make.

By tapping into the wisdom available to you from these four types of intelligence, you create a subtle shift in the direction of the sales meeting. Rather than being a transactional process rooted in logic alone, your sales meetings will become honest, consultative conversations that:

- Allow your prospects to feel seen and heard
- Cultivate trust within your prospects
- Enable you to ask for the sale with more confidence when you need to ask
- Enable you to close sales when you don't need to ask
- Dramatically increase your closing rate
- Create greater customer satisfaction
- Result in increased customer referrals

Affirm your dedication to achieving the

highest good for all involved

Ultimately, all forms of intelligence derive from loving consciousness. This means that you won't have to fear that what is good for you (e.g., closing a sale) will somehow come at the expense of your customer (e.g., that you will push something on them that they don't need or want). You also won't have to fear that by doing what is good for the customer (e.g., releasing your attachment to the sale), you may suffer as a result (e.g., experience a drop in sales). Aim to access the full scope of intelligence available to you and to maintain a holistic, comprehensive awareness of how loving consciousness will lead you to what is best for you and the customer. The key is balance.

I have a dear friend named Wendy, whom I have known since elementary school. Wendy is one of the most intellectually gifted people I have ever known. A few years ago, we were walking around Lake Merritt in Oakland, and I was telling her how things flowed best for me when I was in my heart.

"Oh," Wendy said thoughtfully. "Yes, I know what you mean about having things flow easily when you're in your heart. But for me, flow happens when I'm engaged with my intellect and I'm learning. I feel best when I'm using my knowledge for a specific outcome."

Wendy had just started a new career as a registered nurse—a profession rooted in science and requiring great mental sharpness. So at first, I assumed she meant that mental intelligence was the only way she was able to feel in the flow. But when I asked her to describe her experience in more detail, she said, "Well, the feeling is like when my brain and body are engaged, and I'm helping people. I feel responsive, like I'm picking up on things without needing an explanation from people. I'm intuiting things. I'm tuned in."

Wendy went on to say: "In becoming a nurse, I finally found a profession that allows me to access all of that in my work. I'm always trying to be three steps ahead by using my brain, body, and intuition. That also involves working with other people. It happens with a team. Working alone in the field isn't the same as working with others." Wendy had just described her experience of being in a flow state. It involved drawing upon all four types of intelligence: mental, emotional, somatic, and intuitive. To me, her emphasis on that flow state occurring in the presence of other people meant that her heart was a necessary catalyst for that connected state.

Being connected to loving consciousness may manifest in different ways for different people, but ultimately, what matters is drawing upon all four types of intelligence in a balanced way.

How to access emotional intelligence

Have you heard the expression, "People don't care how much you know until they know how much you care"? Emotional intelligence is what allows you to form this critical connection with your clients and prospects. While mental intelligence is rooted in the brain, emotional intelligence resides within the heart. By connecting to your heart, you will be able to manage your own emotions and respond skillfully to the emotional state of your customers.

Author Jeb Blount writes in his book *Sales EQ*:

Today, the impact of sales-specific emotional intelligence on sales performance can no longer be ignored. Buyers are starving for authentic human interaction. In our tech-dominated society, interpersonal skills (responding to and man-

aging the emotions of others) and intrapersonal skills (managing your own disruptive emotions) are more essential to success in sales than at any point in history.

By cultivating your emotional intelligence, you will bring your best self to the table. You will need to be carefully attuned to what will best serve the customer, while you avoid the trappings of ego-motivated sales. You will also have to steer clear of thoughts of fear or scarcity.

By demonstrating a high level of emotional intelligence, you:

- Can manage your own emotions
- Avoid the impulse to force a sale for your benefit
- Are attuned to the customer's emotional state
- Can identify what your customers feel and need
- Maintain a positive, optimistic outlook
- Form enduring relationships with your customers

Stop for a moment and consider all that is involved in emotional intelligence. It's a lot to manage your own emotions while remaining attuned to your customer's too! Sales is all about relationships, but the stakes are much higher than in a simple social relationship because the relationship is aimed at a specific outcome (the sale). Thus, it is critical to building trust within your customers. If you are attuned to how they feel and what they want, while remaining detached from personal gain, you will be able to create a relationship built on trust.

All the while, the conversation must remain true to identifying problems and solutions in the context of the product or service you are representing. If you focus too much on being liked, or on being chummy with your customers, you won't be able to serve them as you intended to. You also won't reach your goals. It's about striking a very fine balance.

Connecting with emotional intelligence is key, because even though the endgame is the sale and not the relationship, you can't have a sale at the end without a relationship to get you there. Provided that your product does serve the needs and desires of the customer, if you withhold that sale from the customer for fear of being pushy or "salesy," you are not authentically serving the relationship. You do a disservice to your customer if you have a product or service that would add value to their life and you do not make an offer. Your relationship with your customer must be focused on serving their highest good. The deeper and more authentic, the better.

As long as you focus on emotional intelligence, your sales meeting will go well. A sales meeting can really only be derailed in three ways:

- You allow your fears to drive the show—fear of being pushy or fear of being "salesy." (The topic of fear is so big, I've devoted an entire chapter to it.)
- You focus too much on your desire for a sale, without truly listening to what the customer needs.
- You focus too much on being friends or wanting to be liked, forgetting the purpose of your meeting.

Your sales meetings will stay on track if you use your emotional intelligence to authentically connect with your customer, identify their needs, and offer them the product or solution best suited to them. Depending on the customer, it may take several meetings over time in order to establish the rapport necessary for a sale. In other cases, rapport may be established within minutes of initiating a meeting.

If your business model allows, I recommend that you remain committed to building a long-term relationship with your customer based on service rather than trying to force a short-term sale. Over time, this will deepen the customer's trust in you and their appreciation for the value you offer. Soon you will find them reaching out and asking you for your products and services rather than you seeking them out and having to "pitch" an offer.

Four heart-powered steps to building emotional intelligence:

1. Bring your attention to your heart. You can start by thinking of the physical area in your chest where your heart is located, and can even place your palms above your heart. Now, think of someone, some place, or something that you love (anything or anyone for whom you feel immense love and gratitude). Keep your attention on that feeling. Allow it to expand within your heart. This feeling is your portal to loving consciousness. Do this before meeting with a customer and whenever you need it.

2. Let go of fear, scarcity, and your desire for a sale. Can you trust that loving consciousness is there by your side? Can you trust that if you remain present for your customer, you will have the courage to present your offering when it meets the customer's needs and wants?

3. Remain focused on understanding your customer. People have a fundamental desire to be heard and to be understood. Uncover true needs and wants by asking thoughtful questions and listening to the answers. Ask follow-up questions to show that you want to know more and that what they say matters. Just remember that you aren't a therapist or a pal. Keep the conversation relevant to your offer, which, of course, encompasses pain points and underlying emotions related to your offer.

4. Show that you're listening and that you care. If you can show that you are truly listening by concisely reflecting back to them what you just heard in their own words, they will feel that you "get" them. Mirror their body language. Show genuine empathy, while maintaining a positive outlook.

Another way to think of building your emotional intelligence is to follow the new ABCs. I'm sure you're familiar with the old phrase "Always Be Closing," meaning that as a rep your entire focus should be on closing deals and bringing money in the door. Scrap that right now! Instead, follow the new ABCs of Heart-Powered Sales:

- Always Be Connecting (seek to understand your customer's needs, wants, and feelings)
- Always Be Curious (ask questions, probe deeper, and listen carefully to the answers)
- Always Be Classy (put your personal motivations and frustrations to the side)

By following these ABCs, your emotional intelligence will shine in your sales meetings.

How to access somatic intelligence

We don't utilize somatic intelligence nearly enough. We're usually caught up in the racing thoughts in our minds. To get back into your body, simply take a deep breath and notice whatever it is that you feel. When you're planning your day, is there anything that makes you tense up? Pay special attention to your solar plexus (the area above your belly button and below your heart). Do you ever notice a feeling of constriction in that area? This could indicate that you're offtrack or that you should avoid a situation. Conversely, do you ever feel a warming sensation or expansiveness in your solar plexus? This could indicate a great opportunity or something you should explore further.

Gut feeling

Having a "gut feeling" comes directly from your somatic intelligence and from your intuition, which are closely linked.

If you're ever unsure in a situation, or if you're ever confused about how to proceed, you're probably over-relying on mental intelligence, as logical dissonance leads to uncertainty. In those moments, shift your attention from mental intelligence to somatic intelligence. Drop into your body. Go with your gut. Allow your somatic intelligence to override the logical dissonance.

You may still say, "I don't know what my gut is trying to tell me." It's okay. It takes practice. We aren't taught to cultivate our somatic intelligence. But if you give it time, the answers will emerge. If you check in with your body and you're not sure, check again. Usually when you say, "I don't know," you actually do know. It's just that your body is saying one thing and your mind says another, so you feel confused. Just trust your somatic intelligence. It never lies.

Whole body

Somatic intelligence refers to every area of your physical body and health, not just your solar plexus or gut feeling. Look at the whole picture. Remember that somatic intelligence and intuition are closely linked. As noted in a research paper entitled "Nonlocal Intuition in Entrepreneurs and Non-Entrepreneurs" by the HeartMath Institute, "The experience of intuition is not confined to cognitive perception, but involves the entire psychophysiological system, often manifesting through a wide range of emotional feelings and physiological changes experienced throughout the body."

Years ago, I experienced a series of health challenges that I'm now grateful for because they guided me to make some major changes in my life. I had severe hormonal imbalances, digestive trouble, allergies, and fatigue. I remember so many times when I was exhausted and overwhelmed, rubbing my itchy eyes, then being pushed to tears as soon as my daughter (a toddler at the time) exploded into a tantrum. I remember jumping in fright when my husband, at the time, accidentally let a kitchen cabinet slam shut, making the wine glasses clang together. It almost felt like a physical assault on my nervous system. "What is your problem?" he asked, genuinely concerned. At the time, I couldn't articulate it. In hindsight, my body was telling me—actually yelling at me—to dramatically cut down on my workload, increase my rest, and reduce the emotional stressors in my life.

I only recognized this when I got out of my head and into my body. Getting into your body and out of your head requires no time or effort. It is simply a matter of shifting your attention and noticing the pearls of wisdom that your body is communicating to you.

One of the quickest ways to get into your body is, of course, exercising. Even then, you may find your mind racing, so you will need to keep redirecting your attention back to your breath and into your body. Above all, hiking, walking, or just sitting in nature enable you to connect with your somatic intelligence, which, in turn, will connect you to loving consciousness. This will happen naturally when you use all your senses to enjoy the natural world around you. Listen to the sounds of nature, observe the light and colors you see, smell the fresh air, touch the soil and plants around you, and feel your body in motion.

How to access intuitive intelligence

Have you ever been deeply engaged in a conversation with a client and found yourself sharing a brilliant idea out of thin air or a piece of information that you didn't even realize was something you knew? Have you ever felt compelled to call upon a prospect when it didn't make logical sense to do so, and then you discovered an amazing business opportunity that was completely unforeseeable? Those moments are driven by your intuition. Intuition is your classic "shower moment"—when a solution or thought pops into your mind out of nowhere. If you dismissed those moments as pure luck or coincidence, you're shortchanging the value of your experience.

Intuitive intelligence is your connection to visionary genius and inspiration. Intuition is the wisdom—the deeper knowing—that derives from loving consciousness. Author Sonia Choquette defines intuition as "a feeling energy, not a thinking energy." This feeling energy derives from the heart. So to activate your intuition, simply bring your awareness to your heart and think about things and people that you love. By activating the feeling of love, your intuition will become more accessible to you. Thoughts of fear and scarcity tend to drown out the quiet voice of intuition. So by shifting into feelings of love, you will actually amplify the voice of intuition.

Once you've brought your awareness to your heart, you can ask yourself questions about anything, such as which customers to call on or which actions will impact you the most that day. The key is to trust what you feel. Whatever information comes to you from this feeling energy, know that it is true, even if it defies logic. It's no mystery why your intuition hits when you're in your heart. After all, it's when you're more relaxed and receptive, and when logic has less of a grip on you.

Since intuition is guidance from loving consciousness, it will never lead you astray. Your mind, on the other hand, will have lots of fun taking you down dead-end roads and on wild-goose chases!

Because of the feeling energy of intuition, it's closely linked to somatic intelligence. Your "gut feelings" are a bridge between your somatic intelligence and your intuition. This means it's critical to pay attention to what your body is telling you. If you feel your shoulders tense up and your breathing constrict around a certain person, you're receiving important signals about that person that shouldn't be ignored. If you feel butterflies in your gut at the mention of a new opportunity, your intuition is communicating positive signs to you.

Soon after I started my job as a rep with the supplement company, a strong intuitive hit told me that a particular prospect had great potential. At the time, this prospect was hardly doing any business with us, but he was a forward-thinking, innovative medical doctor, and I could feel the potential he had.

I invited the prospect to dinner at a time when my regional sales director would be with me in the field. I wanted to jump up and down for joy just knowing the doctor had accepted my invitation, but my sales director was only mildly impressed with my accomplishment.

The doctor arrived for dinner with two of his assistants. After we ordered drinks and appetizers, I asked the doctor about his vision for his business and how our products would serve him best. The doctor painted an exciting picture. I shared in his excitement, while my sales director said next to nothing. More rounds of food and cocktails were ordered. In my view, the conversation was bubbling with great ideas.

I noticed my director wince when the bill arrived. Apparently, we had managed to make a sizable dent in his monthly entertainment budget. After we said goodbye to the doctor and his assistants, my sales director turned to me and said flatly, "That doctor will never do anything big. You can still see where it goes; just be careful not to spend too much time on that account."

Flash-forward one year, and the doctor had solidly become one of my top twenty accounts out of three hundred. Flash-forward another year, and he was placing monthly orders that were ten times the value of what I ever thought possible. By following my intuition at every step of the game, I see time and time again that intuition knows best.

My sales director was highly skilled at applying sharp logic and strategy in the field, but like most people, he hadn't been taught to also leverage the power of intuition. Still, he was respectful of the way I engaged with customers and planned my book of business. Later, when a woman took over his role as sales director, we were able to lean into a more intuitive, feminine approach. All along the way, I was grateful to be working for a company with a predominantly female sales force, where we had the freedom to approach our sales meetings in the way that came most naturally to us.

I explored the topic of intuition with Jennifer Covington, who is a life coach and business strategist to female entrepreneurs. She teaches her clients to access their intuition through rest and quiet as an important tool in their businesses. She says that when you're quiet and you remove distractions, you're more able to access your intuition. You're in a more receptive state, where you can receive the knowledge and guidance that loving consciousness wants to give you through your intuition. As Jennifer puts it, "The ego yells, but intuition whispers."

Intuition is vitally important because we need guidance from loving consciousness now more than ever. The COVID-19 pandemic has marked a watershed moment in history, with massive shifts in the way business is conducted. Climate change and socioeconomic strain have shown a growing need for triple-bottom-line business practices that account not only for profit but also for the enterprise's impact on people and the planet. The male-dominated paradigm of winner-take-all business is beginning to shift as female leadership grows and draws in a more inclusive approach. Without "business as usual," the old "road maps" are becoming outdated. Intuition can help fill in the gaps and provide instant guidance on the best direction to take.

In a summit that Jennifer Covington hosted, she spoke further about the impact of our intuition. She said, "We heart-centered entrepreneurs will be paving the path in this next chapter because everything is unwritten and uncertain, so tapping into your intuition is where you will find your guidance." The world around us is changing as I write these words, and there is no definitive handbook. Our intuition is the most immediate, powerful wisdom available to us.

As you become acquainted with your intuition, you can play with it in low-stakes situations. When you're searching for something in a store, use your intuition to find what you're seeking. When you're driving and you're not sure if you should turn left or right, access your intuition. Get quiet, remove distractions, and notice what you're feeling in your body. As you gain stronger access to your intuition, it will play a key role in your sales success. With time and with enough practice, your intuition will become razor-sharp. In a later chapter, I will expand on intuition and how to leverage it in your profession.

An important note on mental intelligence

I'm not demoting mental intelligence, in any way. It's vitally important for you to know the features, benefits, and competitive advantages of your product. Study up on these details until you have a crystal clear grasp on them so you aren't straining to recall this information during a meeting. But then, remember, people don't care how much you know until they know how much you care. If you're struggling to verbalize the bene-fits of your product in a meeting, how can you be fully present for your customer and show them how much you care?

You don't have to know every single technical detail of your product. If the customer asks you a question you can't answer, it's perfectly fine to tell them you'll get the answer (and do it within twenty-four hours!). But you should be able to effortlessly summarize the key benefits and advantages of your product so these sound bites roll easily off your tongue (with genuine enthusiasm!). Your customer is pressed for time. They don't want an encyclopedic list of details. They want to hear in just a few words how your product will make their life better. Once this information comes easily to you in sales meetings, you will have more bandwidth available, so you can pay attention to your intuition, emotional intelligence, and somatic wisdom.

Examples of the four forms of intelligence in action

Let's imagine you're in a meeting with a certain prospect who has shown some interest in your product. Your mental intel-ligence (logical mind) tells you that the product is perfect for this prospect. After you present the product to the prospect and ask her for her thoughts, she tells you that she can see how the product would help her in her business.

If you were to limit yourself to being informed by your mental intelligence, you would think this is the time to ask for the sale. But before doing so, you quickly check in with your emotional intelligence, somatic intelligence, and intuition. Your emotional intelligence allows you to detect a slight quiver in your prospect's voice when she said the product would help her with her business. Your emotional intelligence also enables you to manage your own eagerness about making a sale, so you can detach from the outcome. With your somatic intelligence, you feel a prickly tightening in your solar plexus in response to the hint of hesitation from your prospect. Finally, your intuition tells you loudly and clearly that she isn't ready to move forward because she still has doubts.

Now armed with this knowledge from all four forms of intelligence (which you can receive in a few split seconds), you do not move forward with asking for the sale. Instead, you seek to uncover the source of your prospect's doubt with gentle curiosity. You might tactfully probe with something like "I'm sensing you might still have some questions about how this product can help your business. What else haven't we covered yet?"

Or you might offer something such as "Based on what we've discussed so far, it sounds like this would be a good fit for your business, yet something tells me I haven't addressed all your questions. What else is important to you as you consider this product?"

With these questions, you've given your prospect "permission" to express her doubts with honesty. You can then address her uncertainty by providing key data and testimonials. The result? The tone in her voice becomes steady. She settles more comfortably in her chair, leaning in. Your solar plexus relaxes. Your intuition tells you that she now really sees this product as a fit. And she places her order organically before you even have to ask for the sale.

If you had followed your logical mind only, you would have asked for the sale earlier in the meeting—before addressing your prospect's doubts. This would have made your prospect feel cornered, and she would have most likely replied with something like, "I need to think about it."

Tapping into all forms of intelligence does not mean you will always make an immediate sale. But if you've accessed your different forms of intelligence to identify what is best for your prospects and customers, the positive results will indeed come back to you. You will build stronger relationships with your customers based on trust and understanding. They will look forward to doing business with you. You will get more referrals, more often.

Let's look at another example of how all forms of intelligence could apply to an enrollment conversation. Let's say you're a life coach and you're having a Zoom call with a prospective client. Your prospect, Julie, is telling you how she is struggling with her decision on whether to change careers. From your training, you know to ask her key questions, such as what the opportunity cost will be if she stalls on making a decision, or in what ways she will benefit from making the right career choice. This is your mental intelligence asking well-prepared questions. You are also fully present and listening to her with emotional intelligence by reflecting to her what you've heard and checking in to make sure you've understood what her key desires are.

Once you're certain that your coaching services will benefit her, you offer her the details of your program, including the cost. She says she's interested but needs to think about it. You notice that she begins to slouch and her shoulders are hunched forward. In your somatic intelligence, you find yourself mirroring her posture, and you instantly feel the powerlessness in the stance. As you remain unattached to making the sale but committed to finding the best outcome for your prospect, you're able to ask follow-up questions with detached curiosity.

Noting the powerlessness in her posture, your intuition prompts you to ask, "Julie, do you feel completely autonomous in making decisions for yourself?"

"No." She hunches forward even more. "I have to consult my husband in making these types of decisions."

"Okay, I understand. What other information do you think your husband might need to know so you can come to the best decision together?"

In this way, you uncover the real reason for her hesitation rather than accepting her lukewarm statement that she needed to "think about it." Even if you were just following your logic, you might have asked her follow-up questions on what it was that she needed to think about. Yet by accessing your somatic intelligence and intuition, you were able to quickly identify and address her lack of autonomy as the real issue. This helps her make a more confident decision in partnership with her husband and gives you a leg up when you begin her coaching program. You've already identified that part of her challenge in making career decisions is tied to her relationship with her husband.

Lest you think this sounds complicated, it all starts with connecting to the heart (letting the camel carry you, as it were). Let's explore how to do that now.

CHAPTER 5: IS THIS THING WORKING?

In some ways, it's easy to know when you're connected to loving consciousness. Opportunities unfold naturally for you. Your timing seems to be perfect with every meeting and cold call you make. Your numbers are soaring. You feel buoyant and light. You're energized and strong in your body, and you connect easily and joyfully with your customers, family, and friends. Each positive clue and enjoyable outcome is a sign that you're connected to loving consciousness.

Above all, your feelings and emotions are your best barometer. If you feel good (happy, joyful, excited, grateful, calm, confident, etc.), you know you're on the right track. Feelings don't lie. Positive feelings serve as a key feedback mechanism to tell you you're on the right track, you're connected to loving consciousness. Negative feelings (worry, doubt, fear, anger, resentment, etc.) are a sign that you need to course-correct and plug back in to loving consciousness.

Remember that loving consciousness is always there, always ready and willing to guide you, to carry you. It never goes away—you just have to connect or reconnect to it. Being guided by loving consciousness means you have less of a burden on you to figure everything out, as you don't have to know everything, do everything, and be everything. Essentially, it will make your work easier and your life far more enjoyable. New clients will pop up on your dashboard out of the blue. Business opportunities will present themselves to you naturally. The solution to a problem will come to you in a dream. You will find yourself asking a client ideal questions that hadn't occurred to you previously. You will watch with amazement as your monthly income grows.

But then what about the times when things don't feel easy? When your numbers are down, when the customer says no, when your timing is off, when you don't feel good in your body? Does that automatically mean you're disconnected from loving consciousness? Essentially, yes it does, because loving consciousness wants you to have ease, joy, and abundance. So if you aren't experiencing ease, joy, and abundance, it's a sign that you need to sync up with the guidance of loving consciousness. You need a time-out so you can surrender, drop into your heart, and plug back in.

The truth is, loving consciousness is always guiding you, but when you've temporarily disconnected from it, the guidance will come in the form of tough love. The nudges will be a bit rougher. You'll bang your head against a few brick walls. Yet some of our best learning comes from the school of hard knocks. When your numbers are down, you're compelled to become more resourceful and creative. You can learn from the customer's no. So in that case, think of rejection as a redirection. Maybe you will benefit from your timing being off in one endeavor, as loving consciousness was redirecting you to a better opportunity. Not feeling good in your body is a sign you needed rest so you could be so much sharper the next day. As the Roman philosopher Seneca said, "Fate leads the willing, and drags along the reluctant."

Think of the tough love moments as microcosmic experiences. In the bigger picture—the macrocosm—loving consciousness is always guiding you. The difference is whether you disconnect from loving consciousness and, therefore, experience trip-ups and tough love moments as one type of microcosm, or whether you sync up with loving consciousness and experience microcosmic moments of greater ease.

I first launched my health coaching practice in 2012. At the time, I was still married, and we were living in Dubai on a two-and-a-half-year stint for my husband's job as an executive recruiter. Moving to Dubai was the perfect opportunity for me to take the leap and leave my career as an Italian translator to become a health coach. In many ways, life was picture-perfect. We were living the opportunity of a lifetime, our daughter was attending an international school, and I was able to pursue a dream I had nurtured for a couple of years. There was only one problem: deep down, I wasn't happy.

I remember driving to the beach with my daughter one afternoon in Dubai, looking out at the flat expanse of beige desert around me. At that moment I realized how my internal landscape was equally flat and bland. I had lost much of the joyful spark that had animated most of my life. I longed for the green hills and neighborhoods bursting with flowers in Berkeley. Desert life in Dubai was harsh and lonely, even if we lived an affluent life. On top of that, my hormone imbalances and fatigue had grown worse in Dubai, which affected my capacity for joy. As a result, I felt a deep disconnect between the services I pitched as a health coach and my own lack of radiant health—though I did my best to deny and cover up this incoherence.

Once my daughter and I arrived at the beach, seeking respite from the oppressive humidity and heat, we looked out at the turquoise water and the iconic Burj Al Arab luxury hotel in the distance. "Where is my joy?" I wondered silently. "Why do I feel so offtrack? This opportunity to move to Dubai seemed like the ultimate gift when we first accepted the offer. So why doesn't any of this feel right?" I received no answers that day. The water lapped against the sand. The Burj Al Arab towered above the beach in its stately silence.

Once we moved back to the US, I realized I had been disconnected from loving consciousness for quite a while. I had been ignoring the messages from my body, heart, and intuition. When I finally listened to those messages and made some major changes in my life, I once again felt true joy.

In any challenging moment, the question to ask is whether you have built up any barriers to block the wisdom of loving consciousness. Far too often, we blindly follow logic while ignoring our somatic, intuitive, or emotional intelligence. I wish I had listened to my somatic intelligence more when I was in Dubai. My body had a lot to tell me, but I didn't want to listen. I preferred to follow the straight path of my logical mind at the time.

Other "detractors" from loving consciousness are comparing yourself to others, doubting yourself, or allowing fearful thoughts to get the best of you. It's normal to have those feelings, but if you allow them to dominate your heart and mind, you will no longer be open to receiving the direction that loving consciousness wants to give you.

Remember my dream of toiling through the desert? If I had continued to drag that camel behind me, thinking, "I don't know how we'll ever get across this desert. I don't think I can do it," I wouldn't have had the bandwidth to turn around and notice how that camel wanted to carry me. I would have been too busy indulging my thoughts of doubt and fear. Once I stopped indulging my self-doubt and fear, I could turn around and see the opportunity right behind me. So I climbed up onto that camel, and then we were gliding easefully across the desert. That's how buoyant and light you can feel when you're tapped into your heart and guided by loving consciousness.

CHAPTER 6:

RECAP AND DAILY PRACTICES FOR THE HEART

D ropping into your heart is less about doing and more about non-doing. It's about surrendering, noticing, and activating feelings of love and gratitude. Loving consciousness isn't something that you need to create—it's already there, available to you, and all you have to do is remove the obstacles so you can plug into that benevolent force and let it guide you.

Exercises to help you become heart-powered

To complete these exercises (and access bonus resources), please be sure to download your free HPS Companion Workbook at robintreasure.com/workbook.

Exercise 1: The Seven-Day Loving Consciousness Journey:

For the next seven days, make a note of each and every positive, serendipitous event that you experience, such as:

- Receiving an unexpected call from a new customer
- Getting a bigger than expected commission check
- Running into an old friend you had just been thinking about
- Having a beautiful dream
- Hearing your spouse acknowledge a concern of yours that you hadn't yet expressed
- Achieving a stretch goal
- Coming across a webinar that addresses a big challenge of yours

The serendipities that you write down can be anything you choose. There's no right or wrong. Do this for seven days in a row. (Wondering when to start? As soon as possible! There's no time like the present.)

At the end of the seventh day, ask, "What did you notice throughout? How do you feel? What do you attribute the serendipities to? If you had to plot the serendipities on a graph, what would the graph look like?"

Exercise 2: Becoming Heart-Powered:

This is the simple but powerful exercise that we covered in chapter 3 to help you connect to your heart. I recommend

starting each day with this exercise. Also, do this exercise before every meeting with a customer. It takes just a few minutes
and involves just two steps:

Step 1: Surrender

- Breathe and come back to the present moment
- Release attachment to a certain outcome
- Ask for help and guidance from loving consciousness
- Trust that things will work out exactly as they are
  meant to

Step 2: Activate your heart center

To do this, bring your awareness to the physical area of
your heart center. Then activate your heart center by focusing
on the love and gratitude that you feel for any person, pet, or
thing. Feel into the tenderness of your heart. Allow the love
that you feel to radiate outward. Notice the powerful stillness
within your heart. Listen to the unwavering voice of what you
know to be true, deep within your heart. Here, centered in
this energy, you are heart-powered.

You can connect to your heart anytime, anywhere. You
may choose to do so when you feel your mind spinning into
self-doubt, overwhelm, or criticism. You may choose to do
this before you walk into a sales meeting so you can be fully
present for your customer. It doesn't matter when or where;
what matters is the feeling of love that arises in your heart, no
matter whom it is for. The love in your heart is a powerful
energy that will radiate outward regardless of your circum-

stances, and it will create a deep coherence between your mind and your heart. This is true power. In this state, your fears will evaporate, and you will feel no need to strive or force a sale. It will allow you to hold your customer's best interest at heart, and it will allow you to see things accurately for what they are.

Pop quiz!

What are the ABCs of Heart-Powered Sales?

Always Be _____ (seek to understand your customer's needs, wants, and feelings)

Always Be _____ (ask questions, probe deeper, and listen carefully to the answers)

Always Be _____ (put your personal motivations and frustrations to the side)

For more help on developing your emotional intelligence, somatic intelligence, and intuition, download your free HPS Companion Workbook at robintreasure.com/workbook.

PART 2:

LET IT GROW

CHAPTER 7: I HAD IT ALL WRONG

The irony in me writing a book about sales is that up until five years ago, when I allowed myself to be guided to a career in sales, I would have told you that I was the least likely person to succeed in sales. If you had asked me why, I would have replied with something like, "Well, it's because I'm nice, and I have a hard time convincing anyone to do anything they don't want to do."

That answer is deeply flawed. It implies that to succeed in sales, you have to be pushy or mean, and you have to be able to trick a customer into making a purchase. Even though the concept of sales has evolved far beyond the days of the guy in the bad suit selling crappy printers to people who don't need them, there is still a hint of the belief that you have to be "that kind of a person" in order to succeed. That couldn't be further from the truth. First, let me tell you about a personal experience I had years ago that skewed my entire view of sales.

I actually did have a very brief stint as a "salesperson" when I was twenty years old, during my junior semester abroad in Milan, Italy. A few months into my time there, I was short on spending money. So I set my sights on finding a gig that could help me earn enough money to fund my outings with friends and day trips to surrounding villages. Did I have a work permit? Of course not. But my Italian was fluent, and enough under-the-table jobs could be found. Soon I was hired by a company that made knockoff perfumes. I was part of the "sales team," which was a motley crew of young students and housewives who had to sell the perfumes door-to-door in little towns outside Milan.

On our first day, we gathered as a team and were each given a kit with sample bottles of the knockoff perfumes. Then we climbed into the van that would drive us all to a village. After arriving, we would map out our designated streets, hit the pavement, and scatter off in different directions. As the van careened around the winding roads on our way to the village, the driver prepped us for our "sales pitch."

"After you knock on a person's door and they answer, here's what you gotta say," our driver/sales trainer announced (in Italian, of course). "You can't go straight into spraying the perfume. You gotta ease into it. So first you just ask if you can give them a brochure." (I still remember the exact wording of that opening line: *"Posso lasciarle questo volantino?"*—"Can I give you this brochure?") "Then," our driver continued, "when they start looking at the brochure, and you see they're kinda interested, that's when you pull out one of your samples and ask if you can spray their wrist."

Okay, I thought that sounded easy enough. I looked around the van and saw everyone else on my team nodding, so I figured it couldn't be too hard. When we arrived at the village, I was armed with my samples and my twenty-minute crash-course training in sales. So off I went to find an apartment building.

As I walked up the steps to the apartment building, clutching my perfume kit, my heart pounded in my chest, and my mouth felt dry. I felt the last bit of sunlight warm my back before I stepped into the apartment building lobby. Then the massive door thudded behind me. I looked down the hall at the row of apartment doors that were all shut in obstinate silence. "Who lives in these apartments?" I thought to myself. "Will I remember what to say when they open the door? What if they get mad at me for invading their privacy? Why would they even want these awful perfumes?"

I nervously stepped up to the first door and felt my hand tremble as I knocked. A middle-aged matron in an apron answered the door. I blurted out the line I had rehearsed: "*Posso lasciarle questo volantino?*" She looked at me and nodded, appearing baffled by how an American girl could have ended up in her village, knocking on her door, and speaking to her in Italian. As she fumbled with the brochure I'd handed her, I gathered the courage to tell her how I had some special perfumes with me. Then I whipped out one of the sample spray bottles. "*Posso?*" I asked. "May I?"

As I held up the spray bottle, my index finger armed on the pump, she took a step back and exclaimed, "*No, sono allergica!*" Whether she was truly allergic or not, I will never know. I can almost recall her making the sign of the cross with her index fingers, though that could have been my imagination. But what I am certain of is that I instantly felt shame, to my core. And I was rattled by the guilt of having nearly foisted something upon a woman who, at best, didn't want it, and, at worst, could have been harmed by it. I apologized to her, shoved the perfume back in my bag, and left the building with tears stinging my eyes.

As I stepped back out into the sunshine, I felt a million miles from home. I wondered how I would ever sell any perfume when I felt like a slimy fraud. But I had no more money to my name, and I also hated to quit. So after taking a few deep breaths and wiping away my tears, I gave myself a pep talk and resolved to try a different apartment building. I knocked on a dozen more doors that day and never made a sale.

I can't recall exactly how long I lasted in that job, but I'd venture to say a day and a half. Throughout that experience, my mind was swarming with fearful thoughts, like this feels so scummy, I don't know what the hell I'm doing, and I hate bothering people like this. I was entirely in my head and my fear-stricken body. Without being in my heart, I was unable to receive any intuitive hits or form an authentic connection with the people whose doors I knocked on.

Even though the perfume job was short-lived, for two decades I had a total aversion to the concept of sales. The aversion quickly fell away as soon as I could reframe sales as an act of service and connection with other human beings. Fortunately, I was given the freedom to approach my work in the way that I will share with you in the coming chapters.

You already know that sales should be nothing like the picture I painted of selling knockoff perfumes in Italy. Granted, you're driven by the desire to achieve your goals and build your wealth, but not if there's the slightest chance of compromising your integrity, or convincing someone to buy something they don't need or want. You're inclined to approach your sales calls from a place of authenticity and service. But because integrity is so very important to you, I'd venture to guess that at times your sales calls are hampered by the fear of being perceived as pushy, or the fear of representing a product or service that is unwanted or irrelevant.

We'll take a closer look at fear and how to overcome it in a later chapter, but for now, here's the liberating truth: sales is about serving the customer in a consultative way. If you remain committed to the consultative process, you will never push something on a prospect that they don't need or want.

A consultative conversation is fluid. It flexes and flows in a way that makes the customer feel understood and acknowledged. Feeling understood and acknowledged is one of the core emotional needs driving your customers' behaviors. If you have multiple sales meetings each day, you have multiple opportunities to have a subtle but profound impact on your customers' lives, by demonstrating that you've understood their needs, and you serve those needs with your knowledge, assistance, service, or product. Above all, if you can infuse your service with enjoyment, your joy will be palpable to your customers. Your joy will also help you to remain unattached to whether or not you make a sale.

CHAPTER 8: NOW THAT'S WHAT I'M TALKING ABOUT

It was a beautiful evening in September, and I was driving across the Golden Gate Bridge from Marin to San Francisco. Warm light danced across the bay as the late afternoon sun headed toward the horizon, and my favorite songs from The Head and the Heart blasted through the stereo. I was on my way to a first date with a man named Matthew. I felt great in the pink blouse, jeans, and strappy heels I had decided to wear.

I didn't have many expectations of Matthew, though, of course, a part of me hoped he would be "the one." Instead, what filled my mind and heart was my enjoyment of the whole experience leading up to the date: selecting my outfit, appreciating my smile in the mirror, allowing for enough time so I could enjoy the drive into San Francisco, feeling healthy and strong in my body, the anticipation of a sunset date at the famous Cliff House restaurant overlooking the Pacific Ocean, and the opportunity to connect with a new person.

Just as I pulled into the parking lot, Matthew texted to let me know he had arrived and would wait for me outside the entrance. I walked toward the restaurant, taking in the sweeping views of the ocean and its sparkling waves. And then I spotted Matthew. As we greeted one another, I couldn't help but notice the instant lack of chemistry and how the energy between us felt awkward.

But then I reminded myself of a statement by relationship expert April Beyer that had deeply resonated with me: "Let connection be your goal, and curiosity be your guide." It was far too weighty to make a judgment call on whether he was— or was not—the one. Instead, all I had to do at that moment was be curious about who he was as a person and remain open to connecting in whatever way was natural and authentic.

After the hostess seated us at the bar, Matthew fidgeted on the stool and stared blankly at the menu. "So," I said, "you mentioned that you love wildlife photography. Tell me what you love about it."

His fidgeting slowed down as his face lit up. "When I'm out there in nature, hours feel like minutes. There's something so incredible about waiting for that rare bird to appear, and suddenly, the bright colors of its feathers are right there in the frame, and boom. I get the perfect shot!"

I asked to see some of his pictures. As he showed them to me, I was struck by the skill and patience involved in taking those shots. "These are amazing!" I exclaimed. He beamed with pride, no longer showing a trace of his nervous fidgeting.

"What about you?" he asked inquisitively. "You mentioned you like hiking. What do you like most about it?" I was touched by his effort to learn more about me. I realized how he was able to be more present and make eye contact because I had put him at ease by asking him to talk about the hobby that he loved so much. Connecting with curiosity was a powerful way to diffuse the fear of rejection that can derail so many first dates (or sales meetings).

When our date ended, I knew as much then as I did at the beginning of the evening that we weren't a romantic match. Yet by remaining in my heart, rather than allowing my thoughts to run the show, we shared a sweet evening that enabled me to remain in a state of positive expectation and possibility for whom I might meet in the future. Moreover, it was my enjoyment of the entire process (the beautiful drive while listening to good music, feeling sexy and alive in my body, and anticipating meeting someone new) that allowed me to carry those feelings forward throughout the date and on to the next ones. If I had gotten discouraged and viewed that date as a waste of time (like a dead-end "sales attempt"), it would have disconnected me from my light and joy on that date and in the future.

Connecting to light, joy, and love

If you disconnect from your light and joy, you temporarily disconnect from your magnetic power (remember, your heart is the most powerful source of electromagnetic energy in your body). Clearly, you want to be in your heart when you are dating, but it is no different in sales! Sales conversations are about establishing a connection, and the heart is the best place to do that. Imagine how much stronger your relationships with your prospects and customers could be if you approached your sales engagements from the heart, following April Beyer's wise words: "Let connection be your goal, and curiosity be your guide."

Sales is the act of serving with love: love for the customer, love for the opportunity to be of service, love for the opportunity to engage in a way that transcends your objectives (or fears), and love for the product or service you represent.

Now, let's say you represent a product for which you don't feel much joy or excitement. Maybe you sell staplers to office managers. Maybe you sell cleaning supplies to restaurants and cafes. Can you find joy in these products? Yes, absolutely! It's not about the actual stapler. It's not about the actual cleaning products. It's about how you make those office managers feel when you ask them impactful questions and reflect back to them to show that you've listened and understood. It's about how you walk into those restaurants and cafes with a smile and a willingness to make things easier for the managers of those establishments. So in this case, the joy comes from the service you represent. After all, they won't buy your stapler or cleaning product because of the product itself. They will buy what you bring when you walk in the door: understanding, connection, ease, and joy.

The service you represent is the opportunity to serve your customers' core needs of feeling acknowledged and understood. By that, I definitely do not mean you will be their stand-in therapist. It would be a disservice to your customer if you abandoned the context of the product or service you represent and, instead, made meandering detours into their personal issues and emotional struggles (unless, of course, you are a therapist or life coach). Always keep the container of the conversation relevant to your expertise and product. Yet that container should certainly allow for the exploration of the frustrations, hopes, fears, and desires your customer has within that context. When you serve with love, you hold space for your customer to express those emotions at the same time that you keep them on track to identify the solution that will best serve them.

Heart-Powered method versus problem/solution

One could argue that sales is not about serving with love. Instead, they may say it's about offering solutions to problems. Or it's about creating the outcomes your clients desire. In the most basic sense, they would be right. A skilled salesperson will ask the customer the right questions to identify their need or problem, and then offer the right product or service as the solution. However, if the sales call only reveals problems and solutions in a transactional way (devoid of any personal connection or love), no long-lasting or fruitful relationship will develop between the salesperson and the customer. Without a meaningful connection, the client has no emotional association with the sales meeting and, therefore, is less compelled to buy the product or service you offer.

If instead the salesperson shows up to the sales call from a heart-centered place and engages in a consultative meeting that is oriented in service, an enduring relationship that benefits both parties in the long term will emerge—even if it does not result in an immediate sale. Emotion is what drives behaviors and decisions. Emotion is the glue that forms a long-lasting bond. Over time, those bonds result in sales that take place naturally, as a result of the ongoing consultative relationship.

So while sales certainly involves solving problems, the Heart-Powered Method is much more effective than the simple problem/solution approach. According to research presented by the HeartMath Institute in the book *Science of the Heart Volume 2: Exploring the Role of the Heart in Human Performance*:

The heart is the most powerful source of electromagnetic energy in the human body, producing the largest rhythmic electromagnetic field of any of the body's organs. The heart's electrical field is about 60 times greater in amplitude than the electrical activity generated by the brain. This field, measured in the form of an electrocardiogram (ECG), can be detected anywhere on the surface of the body. Furthermore, the magnetic field produced by the heart is more than 100 times greater in strength than the field generated by the brain and can be detected up to 3 feet away from the body, in all directions.

Leading with the heart is powerful. It creates an enduring relationship with your customer, and it naturally lends itself to a consultative approach in your sales meetings.

Napoleon Hill stated something very similar in *Think and Grow Rich*: "The emotion of love, in the human heart and brain, creates a favorable field of magnetic attraction, which causes an influx of the higher and finer vibrations which are afloat in the ether." Those higher and finer vibrations afloat in the ether come directly from loving consciousness.

As you see in my story about Matthew, the dynamics of dating are actually very similar to sales. On a first date, we're "selling" ourselves to our prospective mate. We often arrive at a first date with high expectations of wanting to make a great impression, just as we do on sales calls. On our date, we might launch into a soliloquy as we "pitch" ourselves, forgetting to ask our date any questions. If we do ask questions, it often comes across as a transactional "interview" because we haven't yet established a heartfelt connection.

On a first date, we might also be overcome with insecure thoughts such as "Maybe I shouldn't have worn this blouse," or "Am I talking too much?" or "If he's 'the one,' I have to be at the top of my game tonight." Not only do those thoughts distract you from the whole point of the first date (connecting with a new person) but those thoughts also take you out of your heart. When you're seeking to attract the ideal mate into your life, where else would you want to be but in your heart? It's the same when you're on a sales call. Even though you aren't seeking a romantic partner, where else would you want to be but in your heart if you know that emotion is what drives behaviors and decisions?

Have you ever found yourself saying, "There just aren't enough leads in my territory" or "Nobody wants to buy right now"? It can be easy to fall into this line of thinking, and I've definitely had my days of thinking this way. But if we stick with the dating analogy, how many good dates do you think a person will find if they say, "It's impossible to find anyone good these days"? If that person believes it's impossible to find anyone good, they've cut off any possibility of a connection with a prospective mate before they even arrive at the date. Likewise, how many staplers do you think you'd sell if you said, "All these office managers want staplers that are sexier than mine" before you walked into every sales meeting? Next to nothing, right?

Whether it's a first date or a sales meeting, stay in your heart and enjoy the process of connecting without attachment to the outcome. Your dates and your customers will be drawn to the joy you bring to the experience and to your ability to connect to them with genuine interest.

The win-win for all

Author and speaker Simon Sinek describes a fascinating concept that is rooted in game theory. He speaks of the finite game—which is structured in a way that one party always wins, and one party always loses. By contrast, an infinite game is one in which the goal is to keep the game going infinitely. In the infinite game, there are no winners or losers—instead, the players have a mutual goal of keeping the game going. Sinek applies this concept to business.

Sinek argues that the game of business is, by its very nature, an infinite game. Yet many companies approach business as if it were a finite game by aiming to be number one and triumphing over their competitors. Ultimately, the companies that take this myopic approach fail because they are blindsided by unforeseen players.

By contrast, companies that approach business as an infinite game—meaning their goal is to stay in the game by helping the customers they serve—thrive, enjoy greater profits, and have more staying power.

Sinek gives the example of Microsoft and Apple. He attended an education summit at Microsoft, where 70 percent of the executives spent 70 percent of their stage time speaking about how to beat Apple. Then he attended an education summit at Apple, where 100 percent of the executives spent 100 percent of their presentations speaking about how to help teachers teach and how to help students learn.

I would argue that this concept can be specifically applied to sales. Rather than making the quick sale, the goal is to build a long-term partnership with your customer and help them thrive in their business or personal endeavors. Rather than competing with your colleagues, you share your ideas and resources freely with them, for the mutual benefit of all concerned. Rather than disparaging your competitors, you guide your customer to see all the reasons to love your company and all the value it provides. Rather than competing with yourself and trying to beat your numbers from last year, you embrace the ups and downs of the sales cycle with love for the entire process (like dating!) and how it can help you to grow as a person.

During my interview with Camila Arri-Nudo, independent area director for Cutco Closing Gifts, she spoke of how, in August 2019, her team was the number one ranking team in new representative business out of several hundred teams within her company in the US. I asked her, "What do you think is the main reason—what was the main driver—that made you number one?"

"Honestly," she said, "we were just really focused. I knew what our goal was, and I knew what I wanted us to do. And it was just like a daily consistent effort toward that." They weren't trying to beat anyone else. They had their eye on what they wanted to achieve, and they put in the consistent work to get there. They were being infinite players rather than finite players.

By approaching your sales as an infinite game, you recognize that you, your customers, and even your so-called competitors are all part of something larger; you're in it for the long haul, and you feel an energy. And what is the energy that pulses through the infinite game, guiding its trajectory and the players who are in it? That energy is loving consciousness. It is an energy that has no end or beginning. It has a quality of pure love.

When you are heart-powered, you allow yourself to be

guided by this infinite, loving energy. When you are heart-centered in sales, you show up for your customers with the highest outcome for all in mind. You are intuitively guided to ask the right questions, and you are present with the answers. You can find the right solution for the customer (which is often the product or service you represent), or at times, you offer a resource or an idea, or you give a small act of kindness. When you are in the infinite game, the solution you offer will help you and the customer to advance further along in a relationship, guided by loving consciousness.

Make no mistake—I'm not suggesting that you show up for a sales meeting without an objective and without the goal of selling your product. You can and should have these objectives in mind, and the questions you ask should lead to that end goal. In fact, end goals and the questions that get you there are critical to your success and will be explored in depth in later chapters. But start by showing up in a heart-powered way for your customer. Start with remembering what you love about the product or service you represent. In this way, the customer's needs—and the solutions you offer—will emerge in a way that is natural, easeful, and authentic.

A heart-powered salesperson will connect with their customers and prospects with the clear intention of serving them. Sometimes that service will mean referring them elsewhere when they don't have the solution the client needs.

Is it hard to let a prospect go? Yes, of course! But only if you let a scarcity mindset get the best of you, thinking there is only a finite number of prospects you can reach. Instead, aim to adopt an infinite mindset: there are infinite opportunities in store for you. Lest you allow your logical mind to argue and say there isn't evidence of infinite opportunities, think back to how many times you're experienced serendipitous events that your logical mind couldn't have predicted. For example, have you had a happy customer refer you to another prospect out of the blue? Have you run into an old classmate who tells you they're working at a company you've been wanting to meet with? Serendipitous events are the universe's way of giving you glimpses of infinite possibility. Keep your focus on infinite possibility, and you'll be better able to loosen your grip on the prospects you can't best serve.

Now that we've explored the core values of the sales process, let's dive into a couple of other key energetic influences that will enable you to "let it grow" (as the title of this section suggests). Then in the next section, I will walk through the practical tools and sales engagement skills necessary for your success.

CHAPTER 9: THE ENERGY OF MONEY

While relationships and service are the lifeblood of sales, the money you earn is the fruit of your labor. So before we can dive any further into the specifics of sales, we have to take a closer look at the energy of money, so your sales endeavors bring the prosperity you desire.

Approaching your sales meetings from a heart-centered place doesn't mean you can't earn good money for your efforts. You need to provide for yourself and your family, and one of the factors that drew you to sales was most likely the ability to earn a good income. The great news is that the Heart-Powered Sales Method™ enables you to successfully grow your sales, achieve your targets, and earn a growing income as a result.

Being driven to earn money can be a force for good, as long as your work is infused with love for the product or service you represent and the client you serve. In fact, desire itself—for a vacation, a new car, or just more money in the bank to provide for your family—is the force that will spur you to stretch and grow almost more than anything else.

Setting goals for sales growth and earning potential is essential, and you can even make it a playful and fun process. Numbers themselves have a magical quality. I have been amazed by the many times when I've written down a specific number that felt like a stretch goal to me and later find myself reaching that exact target. I often approach it as a game, like "Let's see if this crazy number is possible." I write it down, then release my attachment to achieving that number. I proceed with the entire process that I outline in this book, and more often than not, I look up and realize I've achieved it. But it isn't really me achieving it. It's me allowing loving consciousness to guide me to the next best steps necessary to reach that end goal while having heart-centered connections along the way.

Viewing money as energy

Money is simply energy. There is nothing tangible about money. The dollar bills and coins we touch are merely representations of actual value. It is the energy of money (not the literal money itself) that holds power. Because energy is fluid, it can expand and contract, depending on the additional energy that we transmit in its direction. In this way, the energy of money responds powerfully to the thoughts and feelings we have about it. Numbers and dollar signs can be a very positive, physical manifestation of your efforts, knowledge, dedication, faith, and service to your customers. How you choose to spend that money is then a further manifestation of your intentions and values.

If you want the money to pour in, you have to cultivate your love for it, but without attachment to having it. You have to establish a healthy relationship with it, just like you would do with a romantic partner. This means you first have to feel whole and abundant within yourself, and then trust in the existence of that money (or romantic partner) before the money (or romantic partner) finds you. The emotion you experience about money will determine whether you have a net inflow of finances or a net outflow of finances.

Lynne Twist, author of *The Soul of Money*, states, "We live in a money culture that demeans human life, and exalts money, possessions, and stuff . . . and makes all of us feel like we're living in a deficit relationship with ourselves. That we have to have more of this or accumulate more of that in order to be okay."

It is fine to desire money and things, but we must cultivate an abundant relationship with ourselves, regardless of whether the money is there or not. Ironically, once you release attachment to having the money because you feel gratitude and enough-ness with who you are, the money shows up with far greater ease. Then, when you feel gratitude for it and share it with others, it expands again. As Lynne Twist observes, "What you appreciate, appreciates."

I learned these lessons from my childhood. I grew up in a home that was filled with love and gratitude. We always had all our needs met—and yet, my parents were quintessential hippies who didn't want lots of money or fancy possessions. As I mentioned earlier, they lived their dream of buying land on a mountaintop in rural New Mexico and building a log cabin, where my brother and I were raised. Once they bought the land and before they had built the log cabin, we spent a year living in a teepee on the mountaintop when I was six and my brother was three . . . even through one cold, snowy winter. My parents made their dream a reality, and we had everything they desired for us: life in the mountains, fresh air, healthy food, and lots of love and laughter. Whenever a stroke of good luck would come our way, my dad would quip, "Yep, our name ain't Treasure for nothin'!" They taught me to be grateful, even for the little things.

And yet, once I got into my teens, I knew I wanted to create a different life for myself. I wanted to travel the world, pursue a higher education, and have nice things, which meant I needed money. Since money is energy, if I wanted to have nice things and opportunities, I had to create a different level of receptivity and attraction. The gratitude that my parents instilled in me helped to bring about good fortune, but I still needed to create my own energy around money because if I carried theirs forward with me, I might have unconsciously turned wealth away. I was also enormously fortunate to have my parents' full support and hard work to help me realize my dreams, even if my dreams weren't always dreams they shared. With their hard work and mine, along with my belief in anything being possible and my newfound energy around money, I began to witness the writing of my own money story that included college, living abroad, and an enjoyment of beautiful things.

Money consciousness

I didn't fully take ownership of my money consciousness until my early forties, with the end of my ten-year marriage. Throughout most of my marriage, I'd had a good income working for the cultural office of the Italian Consulate (before becoming a health coach), but I had always relegated the money consciousness to my husband. He did a great job of tracking our finances, while I preferred to remain oblivious and just do my best to spend our money wisely. We worked well as a team, and yet, I was unintentionally disowning my earning power. I was unconsciously handing over my money consciousness to my husband.

Within two months of when my husband and I split up, I created an account on Mint so I could track and categorize all my living expenses and spending. I immediately felt empowered in a way I had never felt before. Knowing your numbers and taking pride in creating a net positive inflow (even if it's only a $10 net positive!) will help you plant the seed of a fast-growing "money tree," so to speak. Above all, what matters is feeling deep gratitude for the wealth that comes your way, big or small. Spend responsibly, give generously, and then dedicate deep appreciation to loving consciousness for allowing the energy of that money to pour toward you more than it seeps away.

Having a career in sales gives you a potent opportunity to deepen your money consciousness in a very positive and meaningful way. In most cases, your income won't be limited to a salary but rather will have great potential to expand as you expand into your money power. And, as I mentioned earlier, you get to experience the playful, magical quality of numbers and how they respond positively when you are guided by loving consciousness. However, there is a huge paradox to acknowledge: your success in sales grows in direct proportion to how much you love the product or service you represent (i.e., not "just being in it for the money"), and how you love money without being attached to having it. Can you feel gratitude for the wholeness and enough-ness that you already have? Can you trust that all your needs will always be met, as long as you remain in your heart and follow the intuitive guidance it gives you?

Above all, do you know your numbers? If you are afraid of facing your numbers—if you turn a blind eye to your personal finances—that messy, fearful energy will show up in your sales. You will find yourself approaching prospects who don't have the money to spend on your product. You will have your time wasted by tire-kickers who don't actually want to hire you for your services. Once you achieve clarity and empowerment around your finances, your sales will be infused with an energy of abundance and ease.

Manifestation

Marianne Williamson writes eloquently about the energy of money in *The Law of Divine Compensation: On Work, Money and Miracles*. She explains how the universe is self-organizing and self-correcting. It is a universe that desires the best for us. "From spiritual substance will come material manifestation . . . It is a law by which the universe operates. I call it the Law of Divine Compensation."

The material manifestation often starts with a thought. With our thoughts, we can activate or deactivate what this loving universe desires for us. In the context of sales, that thought may be your goal for your sales growth this year, and for the specific income it will bring you. Once you infuse that thought with positive emotion (such as excitement and gratitude), you can achieve anything you want, no limits. "Unlimited potential lies within you, just waiting to be activated by your own affirmative response to the idea," Napoleon Hill writes.

It may take a while for the money to manifest, but if you hold that desire in your thoughts, and apply intentional action in that direction, it will eventually happen. "Every material thing begins in the form of thought-energy," Napoleon Hill writes. Similarly, W. Clement Stone stated, "Whatever the mind can conceive, it can achieve." Along the way, watch for signs that loving consciousness is conspiring to help you. These signs often come in dreams and in real life.

Just two weeks before I learned of the job opportunity with the supplement company, I had one of the most auspicious dreams of my life. In my dream, I was walking along and I found a silver coin on the ground. I continued to walk, and I found a larger coin, so I picked that one up too. After I continued to walk, I found a third coin, and this one was the largest and shiniest of them all. I held onto the coins with deep gratitude.

When I awoke, I didn't immediately remember the dream. But a short while later, as I was getting dressed and putting on the same pair of jeans I had worn the day before, a shiny silver coin fell out of my pocket and onto the floor. I couldn't help but smile as I flashed on the dream I'd had. Not only had the universe sown that dream into my mind, as an auspicious sign of prosperity to come, but it also made sure I had gotten the message by planting that coin there as a reminder in real life.

I knew, in my heart, I did not need to worry about my income, because loving consciousness would guide me to enjoy greater and greater prosperity. All I had to do was set that intention, infuse it with gratitude and joy, and proceed on my path, step by step. Because of that auspicious dream followed by the real-life "wink" from the universe the next day, I had a deep level of trust that prosperity would come to me. This trust grew stronger each time I dropped into my heart and opened up to the divine guidance I received. Two weeks after that dream, I learned of a job opportunity with the supplement company, which turned into five amazing years of sales growth and prosperity. If I hadn't trusted in the prosperity to come, I might have continued to scramble in my health coaching practice, in a state of fear and scarcity. I would have kept my blinders on and wouldn't have been open to receiving the guidance in my heart that told me to call my friend Michelle and consider the opportunity she had just heard of.

Remember that money is energy and responds to our thoughts and feelings. If we think of money as being scarce, it will show up with scarcity. If we think of it with a positive expectation of how it will multiply, it will indeed multiply. If you infuse your positive expectation of money with a comma and several extra zeros after the number you desire, money will happily grow in exponential response to your desire. It all starts with a thought, coupled with an emotion, and then it can expand or contract in infinite possibilities, depending on your level of trust and energetic output.

As Lynne Twist said in an interview with Oprah, "Money is a conduit for energy, and when used to our best and highest good, it becomes a currency for love. Money is a current that runs through every life, like water. It flows. When we try to hoard it, it becomes stagnant and toxic to those who hold onto it. When money flows, it nourishes and cleanses . . . and when we pass it on in a way that will do the most good for the most people, it carries the current of our love."

I encourage you to take a look at your money consciousness by completing the exercises listed at the end of this section. Your work in sales will benefit enormously from your taking the time to cultivate a healthy, beneficial relationship with money.

CHAPTER 10: INTUITION: YOUR INNATE GPS

Let's dive deeper into how intuition—the deep-seated knowing within you—can drive your success in sales. As women, we have a distinct advantage because, generally speaking, we're naturally more inclined to be aware of our intuition. The same level of intuition is available to men too, but generally speaking, they have more barriers up, which prevents men from accessing it. But regardless, neither men nor women are really taught to cultivate or even value their intuition. Imagine what we could achieve if we were encouraged to really tap into the power that our intuition offers.

Sara Blakely, the founder of Spanx, is a billionaire entrepreneur whose success has no roots in any formal business education or even in a solid business plan. Instead, the global success of her Spanx product was built on her intuition, passion, and hard work. In an interview with Lewis Howes, she shares how the Spanx empire started with an intention that she wrote down on a piece of paper, after she had become fed up selling fax machines door-to-door: "I'm going to invent a product that will make people feel good, and I'm going to sell it to millions of people." And then she asked the universe for an idea. It took two years, but eventually, the idea came to her when she cut the feet off a pair of pantyhose and realized how she could create a product that would make women feel good in their clothes.

When Sara first launched her business, several businessmen at a cocktail party welcomed her to the "club" of entrepreneurship and forewarned her that "business is war." It brought her to tears to think of engaging in "war," and so she resolved to approach things in an entirely different way by taking a feminine approach. "Traditional business has been a very male energy, and I wanted to see what would happen if I took a feminine approach," she says in the interview with Lewis Howes. To her, a feminine approach meant trusting her gut and sticking with her intuition. The result? She is a self-made billionaire.

If we define intuition as a knowing that transcends the rational mind, where does this knowing come from? I believe your intuition is your direct connection to loving consciousness. Intuition is our natural GPS. It gives us direction in our day-to-day lives, and it derives its data from a higher power— from loving consciousness—just like a GPS derives its data from a satellite.

Some of my private coaching clients say that they feel their intuition in their heart. Others feel it in their solar plexus or deep in their belly. It may take you some time to feel into this and identify where in your body you feel this intuitive power the most.

The HeartMath Institute has done extensive research into intuition, and the connection between intuition and the heart. In the Institute's 2004 study entitled "Electrophysiological Evidence of Intuition: Part 1. The Surprising Role of the Heart," research was conducted on participants using an electroencephalogram (EEG) and an electrocardiogram (ECG) to measure where and when intuitive information is processed in relation to calm images, as well as emotionally arousing images, before the participant views the images. The study provided evidence of a physiological response to a future emotional stimulus occurring before the stimulus is actually experienced (evidence of intuition). The authors emphasized the importance of the increased interaction between heartbeat-evoked potentials and event-related potentials in females compared to males, which suggests that "females are more attuned to intuitive information from the heart."

Additionally, the study provided electrophysiological evidence that the heart is directly involved in the processing of information about a future emotional stimulus seconds before the body actually experiences the stimulus, implying that the brain does not act alone when it comes to an intuitive response. And interestingly enough, the study presented compelling evidence that the heart appears to receive intuitive information before the brain. Moreover, research from the HeartMath Institute has found that the heart sends more signals to the brain than the brain sends to the heart!

How to tap into intuition

How can you increase your access to your intuition? It's quite simple, it requires virtually no time, and your access improves with practice. The process can be boiled down to two things: breathing and noticing. Taking a deep breath helps to center you in your body. Most of us are in our heads a lot of the time, taking in shallow breaths like rabbits, which locks us into an anxious state. If, instead, you stop, take a deep breath, and consciously relax your body, you will take one giant step closer to accessing your intuition.

Next, activate your heart center, as it is the portal to your intuition, and simply notice how you feel in your body. The action of noticing is similar to surrendering. There's more power in the not-doing than there is in the doing. When you notice how your body feels, without judgment, you're allowing space to connect with your intuition. This is because your intuition will speak to you as a knowing in your heart and through sensations in your body. These sensations can be both negative and positive: tension, warmth, restriction, relaxation, tingling, pain, and so forth.

Again, your job is just to notice, not to fix or correct. The noticing is where the magic happens. Because once you notice the sensations, you can start to decode the messages of what your intuition is trying to communicate to you. If you notice discomfort and tightness in your shoulders every time you think of calling on a certain client, your intuition may be telling you the client is unworthy of your time. That intuitive hit may directly contradict what you know to be true rationally. From a rational perspective, that client may be a "high-value" prospect, but your intuition is telling you they may drain your time or make unreasonable demands on you.

Power in not-doing

There's more power in the not-doing than in the doing, but I don't mean not-doing all the time. Not in the slightest! Often in your day-to-day life doing (taking intentional action) is the most important step to advance you toward your sales growth. But before you take intentional action, you need to connect to your intuition (in the not-doing), so your subsequent actions and decisions are informed by the wisdom and guidance that your intuition brings. Your intuition is your direct connection to loving consciousness. Once you have connected to loving consciousness through your intuition, your game plan becomes so much easier to define and execute, and the results you get from implementing that action plan will be multiplied tenfold.

Have you had days where you're following the route you planned for your sales meetings, or you're going down a list of prospects to call, and you keep getting one rejection after the next? Maybe your timing feels off, or you keep running into obstacles that prevent you from achieving what you had set out to do. I know I've had plenty of days like that. In those moments, my logical brain won't provide answers as to what is needed. So I stop my frenzied action (doing), and I transition into non-doing. I take deep breaths, and I notice what my body and heart are telling me. The answers come quite quickly. On many occasions, my intuition has told me to take a different course of action from what I had planned. For example, I might have planned to be out in the field that day, stopping into doctors' offices, only to find myself making dead-end attempts. Once I checked in with my intuition, I knew what I had to do instead was go to my home office and send out an email newsletter, which ended up generating thousands more in revenue than I could have achieved that afternoon in the field.

By tapping into your intuition as your innate GPS, you will find yourself achieving far more than would have been possible with your rational mind alone. Your ability to tap into your intuition will grow stronger the more you use it, and the beautiful part about it is the immediacy of the information it gives you.

In a research paper entitled "The Language of Entrepreneurship: Energetic Information Processing in Entrepreneurial Decision and Action" (2007), author Raymond Trevor Bradley writes:

Entrepreneurs not only use their passionate attention to intuitively locate a future business opportunity but can also actively shape its actualization into reality by their sustained passionate intentions. It is their greater attunement to an order of energetic information beyond space/time that taps them into the rationality of implicit potentials and sets them apart from other business actors. In short, energetic information is the language of creativity and entrepreneurship: it is the means by which future opportunities can be intuitively located and intentionally actualized into being.

Not only does the author describe the importance of energetic information and intuition in entrepreneurship but he also notes how entrepreneurs can shape a business opportunity's actualization into reality by their sustained passionate intentions. It is the entrepreneur's thoughts and intentions, coupled with their passion, that help to bring the business opportunity into existence. This echoes what Napoleon Hill wrote: "All thoughts which have been emotionalized (given feeling) and mixed with faith, begin immediately to translate themselves into their physical equivalent or counterpart."

To put it quite simply, we're far more powerful than we realize. This is because we can receive an infinite bank of knowledge and guidance through our intuition. We can also transmit our desires for business opportunities and sales to loving consciousness, and loving consciousness will immediately begin to help bring those opportunities into existence.

Think of this two-way communication as a dance between you and loving consciousness. You transmit your desires to loving consciousness, and loving consciousness responds by providing you the cues and guidance to get you to where you want to go. Along the way, remain willing to surrender and allow loving consciousness to take the true lead in the dance. This guidance will arrive to you through your intuition, and your heart is the portal through which it arrives.

CHAPTER 11: RECAP AND DAILY PRACTICES FOR ACCESSING INTUITION

Your sales career presents you with daily opportunities to serve others, and to connect to your clients with integrity and from the heart. Every day is an opportunity to flex your "intuitive muscle," so you become razor-sharp in identifying new leads and being in the right place at the right time. In sales, you thrive when you leverage loving consciousness through your intuition, and tap into the energy of money with playfulness and specificity.

To complete these exercises (and access bonus resources), please be sure to download your free HPS Companion Workbook at robintreasure.com/workbook.

Exercise 3: Connect with curiosity

Before your next sales meeting, ask yourself these four questions:

1. Do I know what my customer's biggest challenge is?

- If yes, what else can I ask to drill down deeper into why it is a challenge?
- If not, what can I ask the customer to understand what their biggest challenge is?

2. What assumptions have I made about this customer's situation in the past?
3. Do I have any fears about this upcoming meeting?

- Are these fears preventing me from learning more about the customer?

4. Am I focused on how I can best serve the customer, or am I focused on making a sale?

Exercise 4: How's the energy of your money?

We all know the importance of knowing your numbers. You might be very clear on sales targets and how closely you hit them. But what about your personal finances?

Is your answer to any of these questions yes?

1. Are there any bills that you avoid opening because you

don't want to know the numbers?

2. Do you have any debts that feel out of control?

3. Are you unsure of where your money is going each month?

Stop! If you answered yes to any of the above, it's time to infuse your finances with some love. How will your customers be able to pay you good money for your products or services when your money energy is messy?

Sign up with a service like Mint. This will help you categorize your spending, define a budget, and create an action plan to address your debts and spending.

Can it be scary to face your numbers? Yes! But trust that loving consciousness will guide you to solutions if you do your part first.

Exercise 5: Intuition game

The next time you sit down with a list of prospects to decide who to call on, follow these steps:

1. Surrender:

- Breathe and come back to the present moment
- Release attachment to a certain outcome
- Ask for help and guidance from loving consciousness
- Trust that things will work out exactly as they are meant to

2. Activate your heart center, and feel into your body
3. Notice any sensations or knowing in your body and heart
4. Receive the messages from your intuition

This will take practice! It's okay if you receive no messages in the beginning. Keep at it. Try it during any moments of indecision. Your intuition is there already—you just need to reconnect to it. Over time, you'll be amazed by how it will guide you.

Now that we've reviewed how to sync up with the guidance of loving consciousness in parts 1 and 2, let's move on to part 3 where we will go through the Heart-Powered Sales Method™, step by step.

PART 3:

THE HEART-POWERED SALES METHOD™

The Heart-Powered Sales Method™ is what I used for years, in the field, to generate huge growth in my territory and surpass even the stretch goals I had set for myself. Use this system with consistency and commitment, and enjoy the results.

There are four pillars in the Heart-Powered Sales Method™ (HPSM™):

- Identify & Align
- Commit & Connect
- Follow up & Own up
- Prosper in Possibility

Let's walk through each of these four pillars in the next four chapters. Buckle up! While it's a lot of information to cover, it's broken down into actionable steps. You'll get the most out of this section by following along with the free HPS Companion Workbook, which you can download at robintreasure.com/workbook.

CHAPTER 12: IDENTIFY & ALIGN

The first pillar in the HPSM™ is to identify and align. This means:

- Identify your desires and your purpose
- Identify your goals and strategies in a concise business plan
- Align with your emotional, somatic, and intuitive intelligence
- Align with loving consciousness as your "sales assistant"

What do you desire?

It all begins with desire. Your desires serve as the initial spark or catalyst that is needed to bring thoughts into reality. Desire generates the impetus and energy that sets everything else in motion. Before you sit down to define your sales goals and business plan, get crystal clear on what it is that you desire.

When I first start working with my private coaching clients and ask them what they desire, they often reply with something like "My desire is to grow my sales by twenty-four percent over last year." That's more of a goal than a desire. So I ask them to dig deeper. I ask them what the 24 percent growth rate will signify, what it will give them. Peace of mind? Pride? Money? If the desire is for more money, we drill down into what the money will enable them to do, feel, or have. In a vacuum, numbers don't mean anything.

There are no right or wrong answers. You have absolute freedom to desire whatever you desire. If you want a luxury car, great! Don't dismiss your desires or label them as superficial. Instead, use your desires as fuel. Just as emotions will drive your clients' decisions, emotions will drive your own decisions and actions. So you must get extremely clear on what you want, deep down underneath the surface, and get as specific as possible. Ask yourself, "What will this luxury car give me?" Then drill down even further. "Why is that important?" You will most likely find that what lies at the root of any desire is an emotion. I'd be willing to bet that what you really desire is peace, joy, connection, belonging, fulfillment, or another emotion in this realm.

My Aunt Mimi had an impressive sales career with the cosmetics company Mary Kay in the early nineties. Have you ever heard about the pink Cadillac that high achievers earn with

Mary Kay? My aunt earned this iconic symbol of success in record time, on the "fast track," as it's referred to in Mary Kay.

When Mimi first started with Mary Kay, the Cadillac was a beacon that infused her work with momentum and desire. To strive for the pink Cadillac meant far more than a simple goal—it represented success, power, and recognition of hard work. It was a sexy, feminine symbol of achievement. And because Mimi had 150 women on her team, her desire for the pink Cadillac was amplified by a factor of 150. They each wanted Mimi to earn that Cadillac because it meant the whole team earned "Cadillac status."

In the process of getting clear on what you desire, you get to be playful and have fun with it. You can feel into what you desire in three ways:

- Daydream
- Meditate
- Write

Daydream

You might dismiss daydreaming as being trivial and indulgent. But it is quite the opposite! Daydreaming is the powerful act of igniting the potential of a desired outcome in the presence of a strong emotional impulse, such as joy, bliss, love, and excitement. In other words, emotion is like a spark that activates the potential contained within a thought. If you desire a luxury car, daydream about it! Feel yourself driving it, feel the car accelerate, smell the new interior, hear how quiet it is on the road, and above all feel the freedom (or other emotion) that the car represents. By feeling whatever it is that you desire as if it has already come into existence, your brain will come to believe that it does exist. In time, this will turn your desire into reality. Then you have to trust that it will happen, without needing rational evidence of how it will happen. Trust means you will let loving consciousness work out the details.

Meditation

This is simply a more intentional form of daydreaming. I highly recommend having a meditation practice, even if it is just for ten minutes per day. Find a guided meditation to help you visualize whatever it is that you desire. Try to do this right after you wake up each day, when your logical brain hasn't yet hijacked your ability to tap into unlimited potential.

Writing

Writing is a powerful exercise. I remember about eight years ago, I wrote down what I desired for my life three years from then. I wrote down in precise detail where I would be living, how much money I would be earning, how I would feel, what my day-to-day life would involve. I filled up pages and pages of what I desired, allowing myself to disregard whether or not it was realistically possible.

At the time of that writing exercise, I was still living in Dubai. As I thought about life three years from then, what emerged from the pen onto paper was a desire to live in the Bay Area hills and have a positive influence on people's lives, with ample time to enjoy hikes, yoga, fitness classes, and relaxed time with my daughter. I specified my desire of earning $100,000 per year. I drilled down into what that meant for me: freedom from worry, a feeling of self-sufficiency, and a feeling of achievement.

Even though we were from Berkeley and planned to return there at some point, I could not draw a straight line from where I was in Dubai to what I dreamed through my pen onto paper. Yet the desire I felt for that envisioned life was sincere and unedited. After writing it all down, I put it to the side and proceeded to execute my goals and plans for my health coaching business. I trusted and allowed the universe to work out the details.

Fast forward three years, and there I was, living in the Bay Area hills, amicably divorced, and I was guided to accept the job opportunity with the supplement company. Less than a month later, I started my job, earning $102,000 per year to start.

What is your purpose?

To usher your desires into a meaningful outcome, you also have to get clear on your core purpose. What is your *why*? What unique combination of gifts and talents do you bring to the world? What is it that brings you joy and also improves the lives of others? Allow yourself to feel all your desires, and then get clear on your purpose so you can channel your desires in a meaningful direction.

Your core purpose is what you were put on this planet to do. Is your purpose to help others find their joy? Is your purpose to share love and light? Is your purpose to serve as a role model for others?

Now how does that purpose translate into your work? If your purpose is to help others, apply that to your work with your customers. If your purpose is to share love and light, aim to galvanize your customers into a community of like-minded individuals. If your purpose is to serve as a role model for others, can you shatter the upper ceiling of your sales quotas so you can show others what is possible?

In your current sales role, you might feel unaligned with your purpose because you might have identified that your life purpose is to help people, and you don't see how you can help people by selling widgets. But you can follow your passion and purpose, no matter what your circumstances are. You fulfill your purpose in the way you show up for your customers and in the energy you bring to them—not in the thing you're selling them. Think of the widgets as a means to an end. Can you make a customer feel understood? Can you light up their day with a smile? Can you help them out with a problem, no matter how small? This is what matters. This is your purpose. Represent those widgets with passion—not passion for the widgets themselves but for the opportunity they give you to be of service to others.

What is your business plan?

Now that you have gotten clear on your desires and purpose, you can reverse engineer and create your business plan as a roadmap to get you where you want to go. Your business plan is where you identify your end goal(s), which should be aligned with your purpose, and the strategies that will get you there. Your business plan will tell you how to be in action.

Yes, be in action. Being connected to loving consciousness does not mean you passively wait for results to manifest. No! You must leverage that connection to take informed, targeted action, which will then produce the results you desire. Sometimes the results will be in direct response to your actions, and sometimes the results will come from out of left field. Still, it's the energy of being in action that brings results.

Your business plan should fit on one page and should be quite simple. Simplicity will increase the likelihood that you will take consistent action, and consistency is what brings results. As you create your plan, make sure to identify these three main elements:

- your core purpose
- one to three goals (these should be precise, tangible, and measurable)
- five key strategies (actions) that will serve to advance you toward your goals

To identify your key strategies, first, answer these questions:

- Which of your existing accounts have the greatest potential to grow?
- What are the most effective ways to help these accounts grow?
- Where do you see the greatest opportunity to find new prospects?
- What value can you bring to these prospects?
- Have any of your existing accounts stopped ordering regularly?
- What are the most impactful actions you can take? (Think of your sales up till now; most likely, 80 percent of your sales are generated by 20 percent of your actions. What are those actions?)
- Of the impactful actions you've identified, which ones bring you joy?
- If you had to challenge yourself to work smarter, not harder, what actions would you take?
- What is the number of scheduled meetings you aim to have each week?
- What is the number of cold calls you aim to make each week?

After answering all the above questions, distill your answers down until you identify your top five key strategies (actions). Which day-to-day actions will produce the biggest results? Is it focusing on a specific product line? Is it enrolling customers in a specific program offering? If so, then what percentage of your workday will you dedicate to acquiring new accounts? The important thing to keep in mind is that strategies help advance you toward your goals. If you start implementing those strategies and you realize they aren't advancing you toward your goals, change them! They are meant to serve you. Don't remain blindly committed to a strategy if it isn't working. But first, give that strategy a fair shot—which means taking consistent action.

Example of a quarterly business plan

(Be sure to use the business plan builder in your HPS Companion Workbook.)

My purpose:
To serve as a valuable resource and enable practitioners to thrive in their practices, so they can help more patients experience more health and happiness.

Measurable end goals:

- Grow my sales by 25% over the same quarter last year
- Attain four new accounts each month
- Help two more accounts grow to over $10k per month by next quarter

Key strategies:

- Schedule four meetings for each day
- Make three cold calls per day
- Send out a weekly newsletter
- Focus on having my top 25 accounts utilize our top eight foundational products
- Ask for one referral every day

Tips as you create your plan

Tip 1—You have full control over your actions:

When Camila Arri-Nudo managed new representatives, she trained the people on her team to be action-focused. If they told her they wanted to grow their territory by 20 percent (which is an end goal, not an action), she had them identify which actions would lead them to that end goal, such as making twenty-five calls per week.

You have full control over your actions. It is entirely up to you to make a certain number of cold calls. Accomplishing that number of cold calls by week's end will give you a feeling of winning, regardless of the outcome of those calls. The feeling of winning will bring more wins. The more calls you make, the more likely you are to close a sale. This is the dual purpose of action.

Tip 2—Reduce goals to smaller milestones:

Christina Gunn, chief marketing officer for her marketing agency, called Brandmetta, speaks of the importance of defining your goals and then breaking down those goals into what must be done each year, each quarter, each month, and each week. Christina emphasizes the importance of celebrating smaller milestones and sets separate goals for prospecting (acquiring new accounts) and for business with existing accounts:

I have learned to reduce my goals to smaller milestones so I can easily celebrate wins and gain momentum. After failing to achieve larger goals through the years, I realized my capacity each day is three wins. One of those has to be a prospecting win, and the other two wins focus on cultivating and fulfilling work for current accounts.

My colleague and mentor, Heather Morgan, says that she always has two main goals: one for the growth of her existing accounts and one for the acquisition of a new business. Noting how important it is to have measurable metrics and to assess your progress relative to your goals on a daily basis, she coined the motto "reasonable progress in measurable time." This keeps her moving forward and enables her to celebrate the smaller milestones, just as Christina Gunn does.

Tip 3—Create your business plan every quarter and review your plan each week when you schedule your actions for the week:

At the end of the quarter, and before you go on to writing the next business plan, be sure to review the current business

plan once more to assess your performance. In this final review, write an honest and detailed reflection of the plan. Be as
precise as possible as you reflect on your final achievements,
and write them down next to each goal. Ask yourself the following questions:

- Did I achieve, exceed, or fall short of each goal?
- What worked, and what didn't work, in my plan?
- What did I learn?
- What do I need to adapt for the future?
- What am I proud of?
- Did I surprise myself or amaze myself by what I
  achieved?

Don't let yourself move on to your next business plan until you address the questions above! Carve out quiet time for
you to do this alone and then review this with your sales director or another peer. The honest witnessing, assessment, and
celebration are what cements your learnings and winnings as
you go forward.

Now, align your thoughts and actions with your emotional, somatic, and intuitive intelligence. Be on the lookout for
any areas of discord or incongruence. Check in with yourself
regularly.

Align your knowledge and expertise (mental intelligence)
with what is required by your business plan. Are there any
gaps in your knowledge that will prevent you from concisely
communicating the benefits of what you have to offer (not ev-

ery technical feature of the product itself)? If so, what do you need to study or read in order to communicate those benefits?

Align with loving consciousness, again and again. As your "sales assistant," loving consciousness will transmit the guidance you need. From time to time, you may be guided to adjust your strategies (actions). Adjust, align, and stay in your heart.

CHAPTER 13: COMMIT & CONNECT

The second pillar in the Heart-Powered Sales Method™ is to commit and connect. This means:

- Commit to your business plan
- Commit to being of service to your customers
- Connect to your heart
- Connect to your customers with emotional intelligence

Commitment

Commitment creates focus. Life presents countless distractions, so your commitment will ensure that you prioritize the most impactful actions you can take.

Commit to your business plan

With that in mind, you want to commit to making the number of cold calls and scheduled meetings you specified in your business plan. Commit to your purpose and make sure your daily actions and goals are aligned with your purpose.

Committing to your plan also means qualifying your prospects. You have a limited amount of time each day, so you want to be sure to devote your time to the right prospects and customers with growth potential. If you dedicate precious time to a prospect with no growth potential just because they are easy to get a meeting with, you are engaging in an activity, not a targeted action.

Christina Gunn explained to me that she has a very clearly defined target client that she will serve in her marketing agency.

With each prospect I am able to get in front of, I can close the sale when I conduct my due diligence in qualifying my prospects. The best thing I have done for my business was focusing on mid-tier companies. All too often, large agencies will go after the big fish, and I don't have the resources to compete with their 100+ agency staff. The little fish are not interested in a boutique branding agency. So we focus on the middle-tier companies that many agencies forget about— the $10M-$30M annual revenue clients.

Christina has enjoyed great success with her agency because she commits to a plan that includes qualifying her prospects in advance. Her plan also includes the right questions to ask during her meetings.

Commit to your sales meetings

Commit not only to your business plan but also to having a plan for each individual sales meeting. Many sales reps find themselves winging it or "seeing how the conversation goes." Yes, you do want to remain flexible in your consultative approach. But you give your power away when you walk into a meeting without knowing the purpose of your meeting. Have a clear purpose for the meeting, a plan for the questions you will ask your customer, and an idea for how that customer will implement your offerings. This commitment is important because your sales meetings are the core of what you do. All your other work (like planning your routes and researching new leads) is essential, but sales won't happen if you don't have meetings. This may seem painfully obvious, but I share this because it is natural to let the fear of rejection or objections get the best of you. It probably feels easier to write an email than cold call a prospect. It may feel safer to create a PowerPoint presentation than to reach out to customers who haven't ordered in six months. You may be tempted to spend extra time reviewing the metrics on your dashboard rather than reaching out to ten new prospects. While there is great value in scheduling and planning and goal setting, they are activities, not actions. The most impactful action you can take is to commit to engaging in meaningful sales meetings.

As you prepare for your meeting, be sure to put yourself in the prospect's shoes, and try to anticipate some of the questions they might have for you. Try to envision what needs they might have. If you don't know what those needs are, no worries—that's the whole point of the meeting. The plan for the meeting isn't about pitching them. The plan should focus on key questions to better understand their needs, frustrations, and expectations.

- Commit to being of service to your customers
- Commit to providing value to your customers by being service-oriented
- Commit to leaving your own motivations at the door

In every sales conversation, you are a leader. As a leader, you must walk in the door with a plan and remain adaptable to allow for unexpected turns.

If it is a new account, you may not yet know which product or service best suits them. That is fine! But be prepared with what you think might benefit them by researching who they are and what they do—and then hold off on offering that product or service until you ask them your well-prepared questions. Their answers may lead you to offer a different solution than what you had originally planned. You aren't married to the plan that you initially bring into the meeting, but you are committed to having a plan and asking key questions to discover the customer's needs.

Recommit to your purpose

Just as you commit to a purpose for each meeting, keep re-committing to your purpose (your *why*). Your purpose is your North Star, ahead of your own goals. For example, your goal this month may be to exceed your quota by $1,000. It's reasonable and expected for you to review the goals in your business plan and to aim to hit that goal. Yet when you walk into a sales meeting with a specific customer, your own goals and motives should take a back seat. Instead, as you enter that sales meeting, remind yourself of your true purpose (to help people, to inspire others, etc.) And remain focused on the specific purpose of that meeting, which is to serve and help the customer with the most relevant need they're facing. What about your own goal? Trust that you will reach it.

Motives versus intentions

As you make commitments, you need to understand the difference between motives and intentions. My colleague Jackie Miller makes this distinction between motives and intentions: Motives come from our own needs and wants, while intentions shift your focus to the customer's needs and desires. She says another way to look at this is to ask ourselves who is running the show: our ego (it's all about *me!*) or our best self (which seeks to achieve the best outcome for all).

Earlier, I shared the story of my brief stint selling imitation perfumes in Italy. I felt sleazy in that job because we were trained to sell the perfume without any consideration for the benefit of the customer. It was all about motives, not about intentions. In fact, that approach epitomized all of the "dirty motives" that Jackie says will make a customer cringe in a meeting, such as:

- Being entirely focused on the money
- Striving to make an on-the-spot sale
- Trying to show how smart or savvy you are
- Meeting just to check the box and feel productive

As a heart-centered woman, you are most likely ahead of the game, meaning you are rarely focused on the money alone. You are less inclined to force an on-the-spot sale. Yet there is one more "dirty motive" that often sneaks its way into a sales meeting by giving the illusion of being selfless: approaching your meeting from a place of fear or scarcity. If you walk into a meeting with thoughts such as "I'm afraid of being pushy" or "I'm afraid of being salesy," your ego is actually running the show. Similarly, if you walk into a sales meeting with thoughts of scarcity, such as "How will I ever make my sales goal this month?" or "Customers just aren't buying right now," your ego is still running the show.

If instead, you walk into a meeting with the pure intention of bringing value to your customer, you crowd out those fearful thoughts. When you focus on your customer, your ego is no longer running the show. As Jackie says, "Pure intentions attract good people and create more fulfillment." Pure intentions, such as the ones below, are about selflessness and concern for others:

- Making your clients' jobs easier
- Helping your clients' patients to be healthy and happy
- Helping your customers build a successful business
- Providing resources
- Providing a fresh perspective
- Being attuned to the needs and wants of your clients

To cultivate pure intentions, put yourself in your client's shoes. Have healthy empathy for their situation or challenges. Have an open mind and genuine curiosity, and—quite simply—be kind. Before walking into every meeting, get clear on the intention or purpose for the meeting with the client's benefit in mind first and foremost.

Connect to your heart

Keep returning to your heart. Always. This is the foundation for connecting to your customers with emotional intelligence.

Connect with positivity, confidence, and purpose

Your energy matters from the moment you walk through the door (or show up on a Zoom call) and throughout the entire meeting. Your energy should exude confidence, positivity, strength, authentic power, and humble curiosity. Your power is critical—not because you have any intention of dominating or controlling your customer. No! Quite the opposite. Your authentic power creates a container in which you efficiently lead your customer to identify what they need, and you respond with a solution or outcome that will best benefit them.

What is the best way to access this positive, confident energy? Follow the steps outlined in chapter 3 (The Way to the Heart). Follow these steps every day, and even before you walk into every meeting.

Pay attention to your posture:

Keep your shoulders pulled back, spine straight, and your head held high—so that you convey a confidence that will put your customer at ease.

Make eye contact:

Build trust by conveying warmth and kindness through your eyes.

Smile:

Smile because you love the product or service you represent. Smile because you've put aside your egocentric desires and fears, for the highest good of the client. Smile because you have loving consciousness as your "sales assistant." Smile because the joy in your smile is what everyone ultimately wants.

It is fully possible to smile while showing awareness and empathy for your customer's mood. If your customer is stressed or preoccupied when you arrive, you can be mindful of their state while still smiling in a way that is uplifting when they're down, calming when they're stressed, and reassuring when they're preoccupied.

Restate your purpose:

Be ready to set the tone of the meeting by concisely stating or reiterating the purpose of the meeting and the benefit to the customer. If it is a scheduled meeting with an existing account, I will start the meeting by saying, "Doctor, we had planned to review products for cognitive health today. But I'll start by asking, do you have any questions or has anything come up since our last meeting that we should focus on first?" This way I've reminded the doctor of the scheduled purpose of the meeting, but I'm also acknowledging that there may be something more pressing on their mind that would distract them from the information I'm about to share. If the customer is pressed for time (most everyone is, especially when a salesperson walks in the door!), follow up your purpose statement with something like "I know your time is limited, so we will keep this to twenty minutes." You will be amazed by how much this puts them at ease! In many cases, you will see them visibly relax.

In saying this, I'm guiding the meeting with purpose and confidence, but creating the space for their needs to take center stage. Essentially, your purpose should be composed of a concise intention related to discovery, along with the benefit that will result from that intention. "My purpose is to _____, so that I can _____ [how you will provide value to them]."

Use a steady, confident tone of voice. Generally speaking, we women tend to convey a lack of confidence by ending sentences with an upward inflection, as if it were a question. Show that you are confident by maintaining a firm, steady tone of voice. Also, avoid using the word "just" (as in "I just want to check in"). Claim your space. An unsteady tone and words like "just" amount to apologizing. You're there to bring value, not apologize.

When I show up for meetings with positivity, confidence, and purpose, it creates a beneficial, collaborative tone for the meeting. It puts the customer at ease, because they know what to expect. They know that the purpose of the meeting is to bring them value.

But remember, you could say all the right things and ask the perfect questions, but if your energy isn't positive and heart-centered, your words won't matter. As Yogi Bhajan said, "If your presence doesn't work, neither will your word."

Make sure you maintain your positive energy when you meet with a customer whose negative energy might drag yours down. Even though it's critical to meet the customer where they're at, there's a huge difference between empathy and outright negativity. I'd like to give you an example of a time when I did show up with the right energy, but then I allowed my energy to be dragged down by the negative atmosphere of a particular office.

It was a warm summer day and my regional sales director was out in the field with me. We stopped into a pharmacy where I had been trying to get our products on the shelves, with just a hint of success, over the past year. It was a cold call (not a scheduled meeting) because the owner of this pharmacy didn't like to schedule meetings ahead of time. I told my regional director a little bit of the backstory on this customer and about the products that I knew would perfectly complement the hormone therapy that the pharmacy provided.

We walked into the pharmacy, and I saw it was in the same state it had been the previous five times I had walked through that door: the two women at the front desk looked frazzled, trying to manage the phones and requests from the back of the pharmacy. Through the glass wall, we could see the pharmacists busy at work, along with the pharmacy owner, who gripped a phone in his hand, gesticulating at the person on the other end of the line. The shelves right next to us in the reception area contained the same expired, dusty products that had been there for at least six months. Clearly, the shelves needed some tender loving care before any pharmacy customers would want to buy the products.

I told the woman at the front desk that I was there to see the owner, and I explained why. She went back to tell him I was there, and I cringed as I saw him shake his head. I agonized as she walked back toward us, with my regional director quietly observing the whole scene.

"Sorry," she said to me. "Frank is busy. He said you'll have to come back another time."

"Okay," I replied, feeling disarmed, with nothing else to say. "I will do that." And we left.

I was mortified to have my director observe that scene, but

he always gave insightful and tactful feedback, so I was looking forward to hearing what he had to say.

"Do you know what just happened in there?" my director asked me.

"I needed to be better prepared with my opening statement," I said.

"Not exactly," he replied. "Robin, you let your energy be taken down by that negative atmosphere in there. When we first walked in, your head was held high and you were smiling, and then within seconds, I saw your energy drop. Be sure you bring their energy up to meet yours—don't let yours drop down to meet theirs."

Your energy matters so much more than the literal words you use or the glossy marketing materials you bring in. Keep your energy authentically positive and centered, while also remaining attuned to what the customer needs. If they appear rushed, state your intention to be brief and help them save time. If they appear downtrodden, speak to them in a soothing, warm tone of voice. If their eyes are darting around, use a visual aid like a brochure to help them focus their attention. Remain positive and heart-centered as you respond to what they need.

Heather Morgan often says, "A strong signal gets a strong reception. A weak signal gets a weak reception." She explains:

I developed that saying in network marketing when I was coaching and mentoring people that had no sales experience. It's not what you say, it's how you say it. If you have a really amazing point to say or something really valuable to teach, but if you say it with a weak signal or in a soft way, people may not hear it. It's about confidence, and when that confidence carries through, they're going to have confidence in you as well. They're going to have confidence in what you have to say, and they will listen. When you walk in knowing that you have great things to offer, and you're genuinely excited to have a conversation with them around that, it will carry through.

We live in a very noisy, overwhelming world. People get distracted easily, and they're often immersed in negativity. Every time you walk into a sales meeting, you have the opportunity to be a calming, positive, confident breath of fresh air. As you respond to your customer's emotional needs, you are ultimately leading them toward that same state of confidence and positivity, even in microscopic ways.

Your customer may exude a need for control, reassurance, authority, or more time. Regardless of what the need is, you will establish an invaluable connection with that customer if you can respond to that need while maintaining a clear commitment to your purpose and positivity.

Connect through impactful questions

When it comes to sales, asking good questions is more important than your technical knowledge of the product or service. This is so important that it bears repeating, in a slightly different way: you don't have to know every single detail about the product you're representing. You don't even have to be the best at whatever service you're offering. What matters most is that you ask your client the best questions. Questions lie at the core of the consultative sales process.

When you ask the right questions, you engage your prospective client and guide them to tell you what they need. After you explore the underlying reasons for the needs they express, you then need to identify if you can offer the necessary product or service to meet their needs and provide value to the customer, even if it means referring them elsewhere. If you've done a good job of qualifying your customer beforehand, you most likely do have a solution to offer, which you will only present when it feels natural to do so in your sales meeting.

In its most skeletal form, sales is about identifying problems (or needs) and solutions. But remember that emotions are the driving force behind all decisions and sales engagements. Not only will your questions help identify problems and needs but your questions will also serve the deeper purpose of building connection, trust, and rapport. Remember, too, that the needs that they express to you will matter much more than what you think they need.

Human beings are resourceful and seek the solutions they deem necessary. As an astute salesperson, you could easily identify a product or service that you think would benefit your client. Yet if you convey the benefits of the product in a way that fails to make a correlation between the product's benefits and the customer's specific needs (and emotional drivers), you will simply spin your wheels talking about the features and benefits of a product. This won't resonate with that client, and they will reply with a tepid "Let me think about it."

The consultative sales process hinges on asking great questions and is effective because:

- Trust and rapport are the foundation of the relationship between you and the customer.
- Questions are aimed at uncovering true needs and discovering emotional drivers.
- Emotions and feelings are the real reason people buy, and then they use logic to justify their purchase.
- When you show empathy and understanding for the emotional drivers they reveal, a deeper connection is formed.
- People are more likely to opt for a product or solution when they are asked to describe how it would benefit them.

I didn't really learn how to ask questions until I was in my forties. As a teenager, I remember being the go-to confidante for my girlfriends who would ask me for advice or bemoan their boy troubles. I never had to ask questions—people would just start talking, and I would listen. Growing up in the log cabin, I distinctly remember many conversations on the black rotary phone that hung on the roughly hewn cabin walls. I would prop my feet against those wooden logs, listen, nod, be present, and offer a bit of insight that made my friends feel understood. Helping people to feel understood was a critical skill that came naturally to me and has helped with rapport-building in sales. But I hadn't yet acquired the ability or confidence to ask great questions. That skill didn't come until I started my health coaching process and learned how important it was to ask key questions when enrolling clients.

So what is it that constitutes an impactful question? Open-ended questions are ideal, although yes/no questions still prompt great information too. The types of questions you ask will, of course, vary depending on your industry, but the questions below establish rapport and connection, and you can adapt them as needed:

- What first drew you to work in this field?
- How would you describe the mission of your company?
- What do you enjoy most about this field?
- Can you tell me more about your role?
- Now that I've learned a bit more about you, would it help if I gave you some of the background on my company?
- How is the current economic climate affecting your business?

Questions to dive deeper into the needs and wants of the customer:

- What would you most like to achieve or address during our time together today?

- When you're selecting a product/service, what qualities are most important to you?
- When you think about the revenue you get from this particular product category, is this something you're looking to grow?
- What is your biggest challenge with [issue the customer just mentioned]?
- What other products or services have you tried to address this issue? What did you like about those products/services? What didn't you like?
- If I can show you how to achieve improved clinical outcomes (or increased revenue, etc.) without requiring any extra work, is this something you'd be interested in learning about?

Any of the above questions can be enough to spark a meaningful and fruitful conversation that naturally leads to identifying a solution. If the solution meets the original problem or need, a sale will naturally take place without you ever feeling "salesy."

Essentially, you need to identify not only what service or product the person wants but also what their intrinsic desires and motivations are. If you are pitching a product to a client who is data-driven by nature, but you don't realize that data is a priority when they're making decisions, you might not pitch the product in a way that resonates with them. That's why it's so important to ask, "When it comes to selecting XYZ product, what is most important to you?"

If you're pitching a product to a client who is an idealist and wants to bring more good into the world, your pitch will be tone-deaf if you focus too much on how they can maximize their revenue with the product. Instead, help them see how that product will bring more good into the world.

Clients won't always tell you their motivations in words, but you can intuit this information based on how they answer your questions. Observe their body language, tone of voice, and how they make eye contact. Do they want to make an emotional connection with you, or are they eager to get to the facts? This will tell you a lot about who they are and what their intrinsic motivations are. Respond to their cues and mirror what is important to them so your message can be heard.

Remember the parallel I drew between dating and the sales process? Have you ever been on a date where the man didn't ask you a single question? If he doesn't exhibit any curiosity about who you are, it doesn't matter how charming or good looking he is—there simply won't be any sparks to speak of.

I remember going on a first date with a man, whom I'll call Andrew. From his profile, I knew he was a good-looking, well-educated venture capitalist from the UK—a huge bonus since I've always been a sucker for foreign men with beautiful accents. When I arrived at the wine bar to meet him for the first time, I was nearly floating on air to be finally meeting the caliber of man I had been seeking.

The conversation seemed to take a life of its own, and as he began to tell me more about his background and upbringing, I had plenty of opportunities to observe him and indulge my own thoughts. He was very distinguished, wearing a crisp white dress shirt and dark jeans with beautiful chocolate brown leather shoes. His salt-and-pepper hair had a slight wave, and his eyes crinkled when he smiled. I melted at the sound of his British accent.

Yet as he went on to share stories of traveling out on the high seas and pontificating on the history of political strife on the African continent, I started to grow weary. I realized we had been talking for two hours, and he hadn't asked me a single question. "Maybe this is just nervous chatter," I thought to myself. "He might just need a little help knowing how to have a two-way conversation." I continued to ask him questions as a way of modeling a healthy dialogue, but it only extended the length of his monologues.

So I gently began to interject a few of my own travel stories, thinking his interest would be piqued, and he'd begin to ask me questions. He nodded as I mentioned a favorite trip I had taken through Jordan at the time that I was living in Dubai. But he reacted as though I had just told him it was a nice day outside. "Yes," he said, "and speaking of the Middle East, I spent a few months there before I was offered a position in Singapore." It was no use. I held on for another hour, becoming increasingly embarrassed at how long I'd allowed the monologue to continue while feigning interest, hoping for one or two redeeming questions from him in order to justify the allure of his accent and affluent stature. No such luck.

As we said our goodbyes and he told me how lovely the evening had been, I was struck by the chill of loneliness that had settled around me after spending three hours with this man. I've always relished my solitude and alone time—so feeling loneliness in the presence of another person was particularly striking. I realized Andrew had spent three hours trying to "sell" me on him. And he certainly had all the features for a successful "close": good looks, lofty education, sexy accent, venture capitalist wealth . . . and yet because he didn't ask me a single question, no part of me was buying in.

Always be connecting. Questions create meaningful dialogue. By expressing genuine curiosity about the thoughts, desires, experiences, and needs of the other person, you ignite synergy and reciprocal interest. Regardless of whether it is a first date, a ten-year wedding anniversary, or a sales meeting, impactful questions create a connection from the heart. And connection from the heart is where the magic happens.

I'm sure you are more aware than Andrew was of the thoughts and feelings of your prospective buyers. Yet if you're afraid of silence, you may find yourself nervously listing the features and benefits of your product. If you're nervous about the thoughts and judgments of your prospects, you may chat aimlessly in order to show you aren't pushy. Stop and ask yourself, "Am I being an Andrew? Am I trying to sell the customer, or can I get curious for a moment about my customer's thoughts and feelings?"

You can list the features and benefits of your product, and you can even tell your prospective buyer exactly why it is perfect for them—but it won't land if your customer doesn't feel listened to, heard, and understood. This should come as a relief because it actually means less effort: less doing, less talking, less explaining, with more listening and more allowing of the synergy that arises between you and the other person. Yes, you will need to do more legwork before the meeting—study up on your prospect and anticipate some of the impactful questions you can ask—but that will mean less work and greater results during the meeting.

Remember to ask follow-up questions to reveal what might be underneath a surface statement, request, or need. For example, if a customer asks you, "Do you have a product with XYZ ingredient?" don't rush to the answer (regardless of whether you do or don't have that ingredient). Find out what's important about that ingredient so you're addressing the real need. You might reply with, "Yes, we do have a couple of products with that ingredient. But first, could you tell me what function or purpose you're looking for with that ingredient?"

When you start to get more comfortable asking questions, you will also realize how many assumptions you unconsciously make. If you don't ask the right questions, your assumptions may lead the conversation down a dead-end path.

Connect by truly listening

Clearly, questions are paramount. Yet it's equally important to be present and listen to the customer's answers. Don't make the mistake of asking a question and then thinking of your next statement while they answer. Also try to avoid peppering a customer with one question after another, hardly pausing to let them answer. Otherwise, the customer will feel interrogated. Your job isn't to go down a list of questions, like a job interview. Your job is to ask just one or two impactful questions and then allow the conversation to flow naturally. Be truly present with what they are telling you. Listen with curiosity and an open mind.

Since 80 percent of communication is nonverbal, listen not only to their words but also to their tone of voice and inflection. "Listen with your eyes" by observing body language and facial expressions.

Above all, listening involves energy perception. What does your customer's energy tell you? Is their energy rushed, anxious, or guarded? Are they leaning in, wanting to share, willing to learn more? By using your energy perception, you will learn so much more about your customer and their thoughts and emotions, beyond the words they're speaking. We all have the ability to perceive energy, so strengthen this skill by simply feeling the energy of another person (tap into your somatic intelligence to do this). You will begin to notice that energy is almost palpable, like something you could touch or hold.

If your customer's energy is prickly or guarded, use a gentle tone of voice and reiterate your purpose in being there to support them. Ask them what they would most like to discuss, even if it's different from the intended topic of the meeting. What other questions can you ask to put them at ease? Are you pacing your own body language and adapting to theirs? Do they need more physical space? Have you asked them how much time they have for the meeting and are committed to finishing within that time frame? This is how you demonstrate that you're listening and aware of what they need.

If you sense they're not able to be present, it's perfectly okay to say, "I'm sensing you might have too much going on today. Would it be better for you if we reschedule?" This question might help them to relax or even to share more of what's on their mind.

If instead they're leaning in and their energy is warm, this is your cue to engage further. Continue your discovery to find what they need, and when the time is right, offer your solution.

By truly listening, you will:

- Demonstrate that you care
- Discover underlying needs and root-cause issues
- Be able to reflect back to the customer, in their words, what you heard
- Deepen your rapport and trust

Connect in closing the sale

After learning what your customer needs, present your product by describing the benefits—not features. Directly link those benefits to the needs that the customer expressed. But keep in mind, your customers don't just want to take your word for it. So if you can tell them about a specific experience or benefit that their peer had, they will be far more likely to resonate with your offer and feel more confident in their purchase. Paint a vivid picture with brief but impactful stories. Tell them what other customers have said. They want to hear it from the horse's mouth. Stories and numbers bring testimonials to life. After all, it's more effective to say, "My client Sandy saw a fifteen percent increase in her revenue after using my service for six weeks" than it is to say something vague like "I get lots of good feedback on my services."

With impactful questions and true listening, the close will often happen as a natural next step. Only attempt to close the sale if you have determined your product is a good fit for the customer. This will increase the likelihood that you won't even need to ask for the sale because the customer will close themselves.

At times you will need to ask for the sale, but you should never feel "salesy." You want to do it in a way that feels natural, and it will often lead to a yes. If you have determined your project is right for them, you can close in several ways:

- Can you see how this would benefit your customers and add to your bottom line?
- Now that we've reviewed this product, what are your thoughts on it?
- Which of your customers (or patients, etc.) would benefit most from this?
- Which of the products we have reviewed today feels like the best product for your business?
- Of the various service options that we reviewed, which one feels like the best fit for you?

- Is there any other information you need as you consider this product?

What if you get the dreaded statement: "Let me think about it"? In all likelihood, they have an objection or doubt that needs to be uncovered. Or perhaps they truly need to think about it, and they don't want to feel pressured to decide at that moment. If you sense that they want to decide on their terms, don't press them. Instead, ask them when would be a good time for you to follow up to get their order and by what means (text, email, or phone call). Agree to that and maintain your promise to follow up on the order.

Let's say that you represent a line of skincare products, and you're meeting with the owner of a skincare spa. You've done your research beforehand, and you see that they don't carry many products dedicated to the treatment of acne. You've also determined that your products are in line with the price points of products currently offered in the store.

In the course of your meeting, you ask the spa owner several key questions:

- What percentage of your customers come to the spa requesting help with their acne?
- What qualities and criteria are you looking for when choosing different skincare lines?
- What qualities and criteria are important to your customers?

- What do you like about the product that you are already carrying? (if they already carry a product similar to the one you're offering)
- How important is it to you to offer a full range of products and choices to your customers?

Once the spa owner has answered those questions, you present the products that are specific to acne, while also emphasizing the qualities and criteria that are important to the spa owner and spa customers. If the spa owner seems data-driven, be sure to include a client testimonial, case study, or clinical data in your product presentation. Illustrate with impactful details, but be concise. By listening to the owner's responses and by observing their body language, you can tell whether they believe the products are a good fit for the spa. If they are in the affirmative, this is the point at which you can naturally close the sale with a statement such as, "Since you mentioned that twenty percent of your customers are looking for a topical solution for acne, and since these products meet the criteria that are important to you, what feels like a comfortable number of bottles to start with today?" In many cases, they will tell you how many bottles they need, and you can finalize the order.

Transform objections into opportunities

If you sense your customer has an underlying objection, do not be afraid to uncover that objection. If the objection is allowed to lie dormant, the sale won't take place anyway. An objection is an opportunity to deepen the relationship.

So then how can you uncover the objection if the customer doesn't immediately express it? Try one of these questions:

- I'm sensing some hesitation about the value of the products we discussed. Was there something that didn't quite suit what you're looking for?
- Are there any criteria you're looking for that aren't met by these products?
- Are there other data points you need as you weigh these options?

Your customer may say that they're happy with the product they're currently using from a competitor. Wonderful! This is your opportunity to learn more about your customer and what is important to them. Ask, "What do you like most about that product?" Remember the ABCs: Always Be Curious. Remain unattached to whether they stick with the competitor's product. Always Be Classy. Don't put down anyone else's product. If you let your customer continue speaking, they will most likely reveal the challenges or problems they've had with that other product, even if you only ask what they like about it.

The ultimate question to ask when faced with your client's hesitation is "What else might you need to make a yes decision?" This question is aimed at uncovering the unspoken objections and determining whether their true objection can be addressed.

While this last question may feel too direct for your comfort, I encourage you to try it out, maybe in a low-stakes situation to start with. The question must be asked with an energy of steady confidence and curiosity. It definitely should not be asked with an air of desperation.

I once had a sales meeting about fish oil with a customer. He had been using a different brand of fish oil in his clinical practice, but I knew that ours would benefit him more, for various reasons. I explained the benefits of our fish oil and the differentiating factors that made ours better. Yet he still seemed hesitant to order it. So I asked him, "What else might you need to consider carrying this product in your office?" "Well," he replied, "I think I just want to try a sample so I can see how I feel when I take it." Knowing the differences on paper wasn't enough for him, in this case. He wanted to experience it for himself, which was a very easy request to satisfy. I got him a sample bottle, he observed how good he felt on it, and he proceeded to carry the product in his office for his patients.

Interestingly, I later found myself in a similar situation with a different customer who was very loyal to a different brand of fish oil, though he carried many other products from my company. After asking him what he liked about the other brand of fish oil, I asked if he'd be open to hearing about mine, and he said yes. I went on to explain the many benefits of our fish oil and what set it apart from others on the market. Yet he still seemed hesitant to order it. So I asked him, "What else might you need to consider carrying this product in your office?" "Well," he replied, "the truth is, I feel really loyal to the rep from the other company. We've had a long-standing relationship for many years, and it's hard for me to stop carrying her product."

With such a direct question, we got to the truth of his objection. I acknowledged and praised his loyalty to the other rep and told him I understood why he would want to keep his fish oil business with her. It would have felt out of character for me to try to dissuade him from that because relationships are paramount. I also took it as a key indication that he also valued his relationship with me, since he had been carrying several other products of ours for years. By honoring his loyalty to the fish oil rep, I demonstrated to him that I shared his value of loyalty, which helped to strengthen his loyalty to me for the other products of mine that he carried.

At times, you will need to take a stand for your customer, for their benefit. The customer may hesitate to commit to a product or service because they're afraid of spending the money or making a change. In those times, you may need to step out of your comfort zone and be more assertive than you're used to—only if it is in the customer's best interest. But even when you're being assertive, you should never feel pushy.

For example, if you sense that your customer is simply afraid of making a change, you might make a statement such as "My recommendation is to start with five units of this product. Once you experience the benefits for yourself, you can increase to whatever number feels right for you. How does that sound?" Keep the tone of your voice gentle but firm, with a downward inflection, even when you ask, "How does that sound?"

In the course of your sales meeting, you can also preempt many of the most common objections by addressing them proactively. Most objections fall into the following three categories:

- This requires too much time.
- This requires too much work.
- This requires too much money.

If your product or service will not require more time, work, or money, be sure to make this clear up front! For example, you might ask, "If I can show you how to achieve improved [clinical outcomes, revenue, ROI, health] without requiring any extra work, is this something you'd be interested in learning about?"

The first part of the question speaks to the benefit, while the second part of the question preempts potential objections. Preempting objections helps to bring people's guard down. Cost becomes irrelevant if you're able to demonstrate the intrinsic benefit, value, or revenue that will result from acquiring that product or service.

Keep on topic

I've met with customers who have a hard time maintaining focus. They want to skip around from topic to topic—possibly because they want to defer making a buying decision. This is the time to stay in my power, listen with emotional intelligence, and use the opportunity to set a purpose for the next meeting.

For example, I may be meeting with a practitioner who treats patients with cognitive decline. In the course of our meeting, as we review the products that support cognitive health, the practitioner may blurt out, "And what do you have for blood sugar support?" Rather than allowing the customer to derail the focus of the current meeting, I keep them on track by replying, "We have some great products for blood sugar support. Let's focus on that in our next meeting, because there's quite a bit to review." Then I redirect the conversation back to cognitive support. At the end of the meeting, we get our next meeting on the calendar with the clear purpose of reviewing blood sugar support.

Emotional intelligence is key in this scenario, because it's important to identify whether the customer is changing topics to defer a buying decision or because the original topic wasn't actually relevant to the customer. It's completely fine and necessary to pivot a conversation when the original topic no longer suits the customer. Pivot and adapt with purpose, but don't let your customer derail the conversation just to defer a buying decision.

Commit to next steps

Regardless of whether you close a sale on the spot or not, you must establish and commit to next steps. When you and the customer commit to next steps, it's a way of ensuring mutual commitment in the relationship. Next steps include scheduling the next meeting, agreeing on a time to follow up, or delivering an important piece of information.

Scheduling the next meeting ensures continuity of the relationship. Schedule that meeting with a specific purpose (agenda). It's rarely possible or even desirable to address every topic in a single meeting. Defer some to next time so you keep the current meeting on topic, and so there is a clearly defined purpose for the next meeting.

Scheduling the next meeting assures continuity in the relationship, and it also saves you the trouble of trying to track them down later. Your customers are busy and so are you. You honor your time and theirs when you get the next meeting on the calendar at that moment.

I suggest booking the next meeting with a statement rather than a question. Instead of saying, "Would you like to get another meeting on the calendar?" say something like "Let's meet again in a month to review the products for blood sugar support. How does March eighth look for you?" In the statement, you're reiterating the purpose of the next meeting and suggesting a specific date.

Another next step is agreeing on a necessary deliverable before they can make a buying decision. Let's say you're meeting with a prospect who is interested in your bookkeeping services. While they have expressed interest in your service, they don't want to commit until you can run a comparative cost analysis of what it will cost to use your services versus continuing to do their bookkeeping on their own. They agree to send you their expenses from the last month so you can give them an estimate of your services and the time you can save them.

Even if a meeting does not end in an actual sale, but you establish a next step in the relationship, it is a success. Along with scheduling the next meetings or a time to bring a deliverable, you can determine other next steps that show your excellent service. For example, a customer may tell you that they need a certain tool or resource that isn't the direct product you sell, but if they had that resource, it would enable them to do more business with you. If you can find that product for them and who sells it, fantastic! This is an opportunity to provide value to your customer while knowing it will further their ability to do more business with you. There is a call to action and a furthering of the relationship in the spirit of service.

Sample scenario of a heart-powered sales meeting

Now that we've covered all the essential elements of the second pillar in the Heart-Powered Sales Method™ (commit and connect), let's walk through a sample scenario. I will call out the essential elements in parentheses throughout this scenario.

Imagine you're going to meet with Dr. Steve Adams, who has been a regular customer for several years. You review your notes from your last meeting, where he had said he's doing more immune support with his patients and that he'd like to learn more about what you have (commit to your plan for the meeting). Before you walk into his office, you connect to your heart, stand up tall, and smile (connect with positive energy).

You reviewed your sales goals that morning, but now your sole intention is to provide the best support to Dr. Adams (recommit to your purpose and leave your motives at the door).

After you greet him, you ask him how much time he has, and you commit to finishing within that time. You ask him if immune support is still one of the main concerns of his patients. He nods and says he wants to hear what products you have in this category. Before you dive into telling him about your new liposomal vitamin C product that will be perfect for his patients, you ask him what he is currently using for immune support (connect with impactful questions). When he lists several items, including vitamin C and vitamin D from a competitor, you ask him what he likes about those products. As you listen to his answer, you hear him list a couple of positive traits, but the tone of his voice reveals that he's not very committed to the products. You can also see that he is leaning in and wants to hear what you might offer (connect by truly listening).

You present the liposomal vitamin C product to him and excitedly mention how the liposomal form is better absorbed than more common forms of vitamin C. At this point, he leans back and crosses his arms. Uh-oh. For a moment, you hesitate, assuming, for a split second, that he's afraid of the price since liposomal products can be more expensive. But you check yourself on your assumption and remember to find out what he really thinks rather than rushing to tell him about any special discounts he can get.

"What are your thoughts on the liposomal form of vitamin C?" you ask.

"Well," he replies, "I've just heard that there's a lot of marketing hype about liposomal products in general."

"Ah. I'm glad you mentioned that because it's true. There's a lot of marketing hype out there, and most liposomal products don't live up to their promise. Would it be helpful if I show you how this product is different?" (transform objections into opportunities). Also notice how your reply mirrors and validates what he has just said, to show that you've really heard him.

He nods. You proceed to present data on the specific technology used to make this liposomal product as well as its efficacy, because you know he is data-driven.

When you can see him leaning in again and nodding, you say, "Can you see the potential for using this in your practice?" To which he replies, "Yes, I can. I'm actually impressed with this data." He continues to nod but remains silent.

You know his patients will benefit from this product, and he just said he's impressed with the data. Yet you can also sense that he needs a small nudge because he's new to liposomal products. Although your solar plexus twinges with a bit of fear in having to ask for the sale, you remind yourself that this isn't about you, it's about what's best for the customer.

"Since this product will provide the immune system support that your patients need, what feels like a good number of bottles to start with?" (connect in closing the sale). In this way, you're allowing him to specify a number that is comfortable and realistic for his practice. He pauses for a moment, and you're aware of the slight discomfort you feel with the silence. But you remind yourself that you have to be okay with allowing him a moment to think. You also remind yourself that if he says "none," an objection is not defeat. An objection expressed with honesty is an opportunity to further explore what the client really needs.

"How about ten bottles?" he finally says.

"That sounds like a great place to start," you reply. "I'll put that order in for you. Also, I know you only had a few minutes to meet today, so we'll wrap up here. But since you also mentioned using a lot of vitamin D in your practice, we could review the factors that impact vitamin D absorption in our next meeting. How does that sound?" (commit to next steps). He says he'd like that, and you get your next meeting scheduled.

Throughout the entire process, you remain rooted in your positive energy to guide the sales meeting toward the best outcome, yet you remain present and unattached to the outcome. Dr. Adam's order isn't enough to get you to your monthly goal, but you trust that you will be okay, and you feel gratitude for the consultative meeting you had with him. You trust that if you continue applying yourself and working within the framework of your strategic business plan, you will succeed.

After you leave his office and check your phone, you find a text from a new client asking to place an unexpectedly large order. You smile and marvel at how it isn't always a linear process of sales pitch and closing. Clearly, greater forces are at work, conspiring to help you succeed.

CHAPTER 14: FOLLOW UP & OWN UP

The third pillar of the Heart-Powered Sales Method™ is to follow up and own up. This means:

- Follow up on next steps and deliverables
- Own your value: for yourself, your clients, and their referrals
- Own up to mistakes

The fortune is in the follow-up

As my colleague Heather Morgan always says, "The fortune is in the follow-up." Many times your customers say they need more time to make a decision. In those cases, be sure to ask, "When would be a good time for me to check in with you?" Get their answer and then commit to checking in with them on that day. Also follow through in promptly providing any deliverables you promised to customers, and check in with them on the day you promised to check in.

The strength of your relationship with your customer depends on follow-up. You don't do this just when you need to deliver information or get an order; you also need to stay in touch to show you care. Trust is built over time, not in a single meeting. You might be afraid of bothering your client or appearing too persistent, but pleasant persistence and caring communication are how you nurture your relationship and show your client how much you value them.

It's far better to be in touch with twenty clients whom you follow up with consistently than to be in touch with a hundred clients whom you touch base with sporadically. If you won't have the time or focus to follow through on a promise to a new prospect, don't attempt a meeting with that prospect in the first place. Instead, dedicate time to consistent follow-up and follow-through with an existing client.

Small actions, big results

One of the most impactful ways that I've built rapport with my customers is by serving them with small actions that bring big results. In general, people are busy, overwhelmed, and looking for help. Whenever I can deliver an answer or help them in a way that feels easy and manageable to me, I see it as a great opportunity for connection.

Many of my customers text me their questions because

they love being able to get answers quickly. (Responding to emails quickly is, of course, important too.) Serving them in this way quickly deepens the relationship because it's more immediate and personable, and you become the solution or answer to their overwhelm. While many experts advocate replying to texts and emails only at dedicated times in a day, and I agree that this is more efficient, when you're in sales, it's all about the customer. Since people are generally busy and overwhelmed, providing quick answers means you've addressed a major concern of the client.

When you love the product or service you represent, it feels easy and enjoyable to answer questions. Take joy in helping resolve small issues or challenges that the customer experiences. Even if these small actions don't result in a direct sale, their value is priceless because they help build a relationship based on trust and a feeling of closeness.

Also be sure to take note of your customer's interests, desires, and anything else that comes up in conversations. Take a mental note, but also write those notes in your CRM (customer relationship management system) if possible, even if the details seem irrelevant at the time. In the future, those small details may matter a lot when a certain opportunity presents itself, or when you can refer back to those personal details in future conversations.

Many times I've had a customer tell me that they're looking to hire a new staff member. So I take a few moments to learn more about the qualities they're looking for. Twice now I've been able to think of exactly the right person for that job, and in both cases, it resulted in very positive, long-lasting working relationships. My customers have thanked me profusely for connecting them to the candidates, and the candidates have been grateful for the job opportunity and career growth. It took very little time on my part—just a few moments of engaging in conversation and then reaching out to the contacts I had in mind for the job. Sure, it had almost nothing to do with selling more products to my customers, yet it served to strengthen the relationships tremendously. Ultimately, it did also help my sales because their new staff member gained helpful insight into knowing what the customer needed.

Just as small actions bring big results, small wins lead to big wins. If you have determined that a customer has great growth potential, don't feel defeated if you only start with a small win (a small sale). Keep proving the value you offer, and the small wins will lead to big wins.

When Christina Gunn first pitched her marketing services to a solar integrator's CEO, Christina was challenged because the CEO had never spent any funds on marketing up to that point. She asked the CEO what their average deal size was ($30K). She then confirmed with him that they were averaging six new projects per month at that time.

Knowing that the CEO was skeptical about marketing, she pitched him a website project at her normal rate but also greatly reduced the fee for her SEO work in exchange for a 5 percent sales commission for new leads coming in from the website. In just the first three months after the website and SEO launch, the company averaged 112 leads, which was a

1,886 percent increase in new business for the company.

As impressive as that was, it was a small win for her in terms of revenue. Christina's agency went on to do many more marketing campaigns for the company. And the ultimate win was when her client merged with five other companies, and the parent company was taking the new company public on the NASDAQ exchange. Christina's agency was chosen to rebrand all five companies into a single brand, launch their new website and investor site, and prepare them for the public trade launch. Now that was a big win.

Own your value

Even though your relationships hinge on follow-through and service, be sure to own the value of your own time. You should always help a client with a quick resource or question, even if it isn't directly tied to closing a sale, but think carefully before taking on larger projects that take more than a few minutes to execute. Be sure to assess the ROI for your time invested. With time-consuming projects, assess whether it will likely directly increase your sales. If yes, it is worth doing.

If not, don't take it on thinking it will deepen your rapport for the future. Rapport deepening comes from direct contact with the customer and from the immediacy of your helpfulness and service. If you take on a project that will require hours in front of your computer (not in front of the customer), the customer may not even realize how much work you put into that project. For this reason, it's the small actions that bring big results. Helping your customers quickly and earnestly with their various needs over time is what strengthens the relationship the most, not the big projects.

In meetings, protect your time from a customer who just wants to ramble. My Aunt Mimi told me a funny story of how Mary Kay (the actual founder of the company) had a trick up her sleeve to help protect her time. Mary Kay had installed a fake doorbell button on her desk in her home office. If she was ever on a phone call with a customer who was gabbing non-stop, she would push that button to ring the bell and then exclaim, "Oh, someone's at the door. I'm so sorry, but I have to run!"

Own your value every time you reach out to your customer. Describe the value you offer in clear and concise terms. For example, say, "I'd like to let you know about this new program we have that will help you save hours of time and add twenty percent to your bottom line." Avoid weak phrases like "I just wanted to check in" or "I just wanted to introduce myself as your new rep." They're already busy and overwhelmed. They'll perceive your offer to "check in" as a waste of their time. Lead with your value. Cut to the chase of how you can save them time, money, or work.

Above all, own the value of who you are as a person. Let your authentic self shine. Be professional, but don't try to conform to how you think you "should" be. With loving consciousness as your "sales assistant," you will naturally bring more joy, reassurance, and kindness into their day. No one else can do that in exactly the way you can.

One degree of separation

Own your value by asking for referrals. Referrals are the number one best way to obtain new business because you are just one degree away from your next great lead. Don't shy away from asking your existing customers for referrals to other prospects, especially in a moment when they're telling you how happy they've been with your product or service. Own your value, and remind them of the value you can bring to others. Say something like, "Your happiness and satisfaction mean the world to me. Thank you. If you know someone else who could also benefit from what I provide, please do let me know."

Help jog their memory by concisely describing the kind of client you're seeking. For example, if you're a bookkeeper, you might say, "Do you know any other small-business owners in this area who might be overwhelmed with trying to manage the books themselves?" Be descriptive yet concise so you can help them think of a referral who might not have come to mind otherwise.

In the course of a sales meeting, your customer may naturally mention a colleague or friend in relation to another topic. You may say something like, "Is that someone who might also benefit from using this product (or service)?"

One overlooked opportunity to own your value and get referrals is when you're speaking to a prospect who isn't a good fit or who simply won't buy your product or service at this time. You'd be surprised at how effective it can be to say, "I understand this isn't a good fit for you at this time. But now that I've had a chance to tell you a bit about this product, do you know any other friends, colleagues, business owners who could benefit from it?"

Once your client does have someone in mind, ask them for permission to mention their name when you reach out to the new prospect. Since you've been referred by someone they know, the prospect is more likely to trust you. The prospects have also been pre-qualified by the person who referred them, so they're more likely to be a match.

Own up to mistakes!

Mistakes are actually a wonderful opportunity to demonstrate your integrity and commitment to the customer. Everyone looks great when things are going as planned. The question is, how do you show up when things go haywire? Are you able to apologize and resolve the issue regardless of whether the fault was yours? While your initial impulse may be to cover up mistakes, remind yourself that it isn't about you. Your focus should be on how your customer feels. Your customers will appreciate your diligence and honesty in righting a wrong, and your relationship will end up stronger than before the mistake occurred.

If you don't know the answer to a question, don't fake it! Your customer can tell when you're bluffing, and it instantly erodes their trust in you. Instead, tell them you don't know and commit to finding them the answer. It's okay if you don't know every technical detail; just be sure to get that info to them as soon as possible. They will appreciate your follow-up and diligence, as well as your honesty.

CHAPTER 15: PROSPER IN POSSIBILITY

The fourth pillar of the Heart-Powered Sales Method™ is to prosper in possibility. This is where you get to enjoy the benefits of your work and of being connected to loving consciousness. Prosper in possibility means to:

- Prosper in money, love, and health
- Cultivate the power of possibility
- Practice gratitude
- Witness the interconnectedness of all things

Prosper in money, love, and joy

By remaining consistently dedicated to the first three pillars of the HPSM™, you will begin to see your prosperity expand. And as it does, relish each bump up in your income, no matter how big or small. Don't wait to feel prosperous. You may have a larger goal that you haven't hit yet, but enjoy the prosperity you have right now. It is the feeling of prosperity that will bring you even more wealth down the road.

And, of course, your prosperity isn't limited to your bank account. Are you wealthy in love? Do you have friends and family that enrich your life? Have you been cultivating a love for your clients and the work you do for them? It would be impossible to assign a financial value to your relationships, but if you could, I bet they would be worth millions. If you include these "millions" in your feeling of prosperity, can you see how your cup runs over? Can you relish how incredibly abundant your life is right now?

When you think of the money you still want to earn, remember that the physical money means nothing. You want the feeling it will give you. So what is it that you want? Joy? Freedom? Spaciousness? Ease? Can you notice all the joy, freedom, spaciousness, and ease you have right now? It's okay to want more of that, but focus on those feelings that you do already have right now.

Celebrate your wins

Every chance you get, celebrate your wins. If your goal today is to make ten phone calls, and you succeed in doing so by the end of the day, celebrate! It doesn't matter what came out of those ten calls. The point is that you fulfilled your commitment to yourself. As you make this a regular habit, you will have more and more reasons to celebrate. You will empower yourself to achieve more with greater ease, and your efforts will have a greater payoff.

Health is wealth

Can you appreciate how much more difficult it is to access your intuition and mental intelligence if you're tired, hungry, thirsty, or sluggish? It is much more challenging to be attuned to your clients' emotional state if you're depleted or foggy-headed. While we look for methods and strategies to close deals, we neglect to remember that health is wealth. Your physical health is a priceless asset, and it will fuel your ability to access business opportunities far more quickly than any new sales tactic can. Therefore, you must nurture your body with about eight hours of sleep each night, daily exercise (ideally in nature), clean water, and whole foods nutrition.

By nurturing your health, you also own your beauty. When you feel healthy and strong in your body, you project confidence.

Embrace your femininity

Your physical health also projects into your appearance and femininity. Whatever your style of clothes and makeup, make sure it aligns with your identity while also projecting professionalism. Your appearance—and more importantly your energy and vitality—matter a great deal to your customers, whether you like it or not. Make sure you can project the best of yourself.

In a profession that has commonly been more male-dominated, don't bother trying to be like men. Embrace the gifts you have as a woman. Your femininity means so many things, starting with receptivity, awareness, fluidity, and intuition. Receptivity is key because the universe is continually putting opportunities in your path. By receiving and listening, you can reduce your energy output and increase the abundance that comes to you. This doesn't mean being passive. Your work still does require proactivity and effort, but the key is to strike a healthy balance in the areas of:

- Giving and receiving
- Doing and allowing
- Action and non-action
- Working and resting

Diversify your assets

Just as a wise investor diversifies their investments, remember to diversify your efforts. Keep cultivating and growing your existing accounts while also searching for new prospects (as long as you can provide consistent follow-up). As you plan your sales engagements, be sure to have a goal for reaching out to a certain percentage of each type of account (and to a certain percentage of new accounts versus existing accounts) so your focus isn't weighted too heavily in one area at the expense of another. Think of your book of business as a bouquet of flowers, rich in various colors.

Cultivate the power of possibility

You never know where your next client or customer will come from. If you're open to possibility every day, and if you engage with people freely and openly without attachment to the outcome, new clients can present themselves to you when you least expect it. Do you recall the story I shared about my Aunt Mimi, who had a successful career with Mary Kay? Part of her success was because of her openness to speak to people wherever she went. As a result, she became the highest-earning recruit on her team. Then Mimi became the first spin-off director. Mimi's mantra has always been, "If you don't ask, it's an automatic no." Everywhere she goes, she's open to the possibility that she may find a new connection. As a result, she often experiences serendipitous events and makes fortuitous connections. If you're too busy feeling frustrated about the last client who said no, you won't notice the new prospect standing right in front of you.

Every possibility exists for you

Beyond each microcosmic possibility, you have a greater macrocosm of possibility always available to you. Loving consciousness offers every possibility for you as pure potential. What determines the actualization (manifestation) of that possibility is your mindset. If you can think it, dream it, and feel it into existence, it will be yours. Anything is possible. Truly. The key is to keep your thoughts and feelings focused on what you do want. If you want to exceed your quota by 10 percent, keep focusing on how you will feel as if you've already hit that goal. Think it, visualize it, feel it, and stay in action. (If instead, you focus on the delta between where you are now and your ultimate goal, you will stay mired in a feeling of lack and deficiency. This will make it much harder to reach your goal.)

During my time as a sales rep, the company expanded the geographic size of my territory beyond what it was when I first started. My book of business essentially doubled overnight. I could not have foreseen this possibility. It was an enormous opportunity that I was grateful to receive—and I also knew it was an enormous responsibility to keep growing those accounts. All the while, I kept focusing on being of service, having the *feeling* of success, and having the awareness of unlimited possibilities.

Yes, the possibility exists that you could fail to reach your goal. The possibility also exists that you will reach your goal. The question is, which possibility will you choose to focus on?

Engage in possibility thinking

To train your mind to recognize the best business opportunities, engage in possibility thinking. Possibility thinking recognizes that loving consciousness offers an infinite number of opportunities and solutions if only one has the right mindset to see them. Fearful thinking will prevent you from recognizing the best opportunities, even if they're right in front of you.

To implement possibility thinking, ask yourself questions that are intentionally designed to open your mind to viewing things in a new way. For example, when the economy is struggling, you might easily worry about how you can make a sale when your clients are just trying to stay afloat (fearful thinking). But rather than dwelling in those fearful thoughts, you engage in possibility thinking and ask, "Who in my territory is ready to buy my product right now so they can thrive in their business?" With this question, you're training your mind to acknowledge the possibility of a client who is ready to buy, allowing you to actually recognize that client when the opportunity arises. If you remained focused on your fearful, worrisome thoughts, you might not even recognize that client if they walked right up to you.

Additional examples of possibility thinking questions:

- If I knew the answer to this problem, what would it be?
- If I could only take one action toward hitting this goal, what would I choose?
- If there's one person right now who can give me the guidance I need, who would it be?
- If I knew it was 100 percent possible to double my income next year without overworking, what would I need to do in order to make that happen?
- If I allow loving consciousness to help me resolve this current situation, what would loving consciousness tell me?

- If I knew there was one prospect out there waiting to become a VIP client, how would I find them?

Gratitude: the best practice of all

The best practice of all is gratitude. It is the key to creating a life that you love. Gratitude and appreciation for anything—big or small—is the energy that brings more goodness, tenfold. My heart often swells with gratitude for my little cottage, the life I've created for myself, and my daughter. It's nothing lavish, here in the Bay Area where the cost of living is astronomical, but it's cozy and full of love and charm—all by my own design in co-creation with loving consciousness. I feel deep gratitude in my heart for everything that I already have, and for everything that is yet to come. The energy of gratitude is buoyant, radiant, and expansive. It attracts more abundance and goodness with it.

If you agree with Napoleon Hill that desire is the starting point of all achievement, gratitude is the crowning point of achievement. When you make a big sale, or when you reach your growth goals, or when you receive that paycheck, be sure to pause and feel deep gratitude for what you are receiving. Genuine gratitude is a deep thankfulness and celebration of the abundance and goodness in your daily life.

Gratitude ensures your humility, too, because it is a recognition that no matter how hard you worked, no matter what effort you put into attaining that good fortune, you have co-created that goodness with the guidance and support of loving consciousness. Without gratitude, good fortune will dry up like a faucet that has turned off. And gratitude must be felt and expressed without any attachment or expectation of receiving more good fortune.

You should create a small ritual or practice of gratitude, as well as feeling gratitude at random moments throughout the day. For your gratitude ritual, you might write down what you are grateful for in a journal every evening. In addition to that ritual, simply notice all the specific, wonderful things to be grateful for as you live your life. Notice how much you love the layout of your kitchen and feel gratitude. Pause and take note of how much you enjoy your conversations with a particular client and feel gratitude. As you drive to your next sales meeting, feel gratitude for those few moments alone when you can listen to good music and gather your thoughts.

We all have limitless opportunities to feel grateful. In fact, you could spend an entire day feeling gratitude for every good fortune in your life, and you would still only scratch the surface. Get playful with it. Have fun noticing how many times throughout the day you can devote a thought to thankfulness. It requires no time—simply an impulse of energy and thought devoted to the good things in your life, and the good things that haven't yet manifested.

It's especially important to feel gratitude in the challenging times, when bad things happen. You can either choose to dwell on the negative aspects of an event, which keeps you stuck in that cycle of struggle, or you can identify the good things present even within that challenge, so you can quickly get back to a state of positivity and flow.

Let's say you have a brief meeting with a prospect who rudely shuts you down and says they don't need your product. You could let this ruin your day. You may even let it affect your confidence in your professional skills and who you are as a person. But the quickest way to shift out of that awful feeling (we've all been there) is to start thinking of everything you're grateful for. You're grateful for all the other clients who appreciate your service. You're grateful for this beautiful day, which you can enjoy more of because the rude prospect cut the meeting short. You're grateful knowing that unlimited possibilities exist for you, and tomorrow is a new day to tap into that unrealized potential.

In the early days of the COVID-19 pandemic, I leaned into gratitude even more. The days were long, the future was uncertain, and the economy was faltering. I was acutely aware of how fortunate I was to be working while thousands were losing their jobs each week. One evening my dear friend Michelle held a video dance party online to celebrate her birthday since an in-person party was out of the question. As we each popped into our little Brady Bunch squares and Katy Perry thumped through the speakers, it was a moment I'll never forget. My daughter, Grace, bounced to the music with her fun-loving kitten in her arms, and I was overjoyed by the simple feeling of dancing and celebrating my beloved friend's birthday on a Saturday night. I looked around our cozy cottage, with the little gas stove emitting its atmospheric wood fire glow, and took in the lavender scent from our essential oil diffuser.

I was bursting with joy and pride. I was doing it! I was doing life, with a beautiful little cottage that I could call home. With my daughter, who at that moment was able to share in the simple joy of dancing with me. With the scent of a cake we had baked together that afternoon. While I was thriving in my work.

Gratitude welled up within me. Thank you, loving consciousness. Thank you for keeping us safe and healthy. Thank you for the opportunity to help other people. Thank you for reminding me just how precious every moment is.

Sales is a profession that gives you ample opportunity to express gratitude. For most of us on a commission plan, the abundance of income isn't fixed. The numbers are variable, and they will swell in response to gratitude, or they will contract in response to fear, worry, or a feeling of lack. Yes, of course, the dollars you earn will be directly influenced by your dedication, hard work, skill, and talent. Yet it's the energy underlying all of that dedication, hard work, skill, and talent that will determine how your wealth manifests. If you infuse your work with an energy of gratitude and thankfulness for every good fortune, synchronicity, and positive event, the abundance of the numbers will flow. Your career in sales provides you with countless opportunities to witness the evidence of how impactful gratitude is. The variability of the numbers acts as a barometer providing a positive feedback loop into your good fortune.

Even when—and especially when—you experience a down cycle in your sales, you can still find plenty of opportunities to express gratitude. If you choose to focus on the stress and worry of how your numbers are down, it will bring you down further. If instead you focus on what you are grateful for, and you roll up your sleeves and do the work, your numbers will bounce back.

Essentially, gratitude creates the win, regardless of the scenario. Sometimes that win will directly manifest as a bigger paycheck, and sometimes that will simply come as a feeling of love and positivity.

Witness the interconnectedness of all things

The conventional, male-dominated approach to sales can feel adversarial as if it's you against your client and you against your competitors. So doesn't it come as a relief to know it doesn't have to be that way? You can make a sale and do it in a way that brings a feeling of benefit and connection to your client. By connecting to your heart and joining forces with loving consciousness, you will create win-win outcomes for yourself and your clients. You will be able to release attachment to any particular sale because you will trust in all things being connected.

Even when it comes to your competition, think of them as your friend, not a foe. When a clothing store opens on a street corner, the clothing store next door can celebrate that more shoppers will show up. Never bad-talk your competition—it's foul play! Take the high road and focus on the positive benefits of your own product or service. If a customer mentions that they use a competitor's product, this is a great opportunity, not to bash the competitor but to find out more about what your customer likes and dislikes.

Think big. There are unlimited possibilities out there. If this particular client is better served by a competitor, view your meeting as an opportunity to ask for a referral rather than a direct sale. Remember to think in terms of the infinite game, in which the ultimate goal is the mutual benefit of all, rather than thinking of it in terms of winners and losers.

CHAPTER 16: FOR COACHES AND HEALTHCARE PRACTITIONERS

Although I've written this book primarily for women in sales, this material can easily be applied to coaches and healthcare practitioners. If you are a coach or healthcare practitioner, you most likely think of yourself as a healer, which, of course, you are. But you are also in sales. The livelihood of your practice depends on your ability to enroll clients and patients into your practice. If you can't enroll them, you can't help them. If you can't help them, you can't keep your doors open. It's as simple as that.

By now I'm sure you've absorbed my message that sales is about service. Hopefully, this will help dispel any fear you may have about sales. The moment you engage with a prospective client who is considering your programs, you are serving them by determining whether your program is a good fit for their needs. If they enroll, your coaching or healing services are a continuation of that initial conversation.

Just like I have outlined, your initial enrollment conversation should be approached in a spirit of discovery and curiosity. Remember, the most important thing you can do is to ask impactful questions. The point of the questions is to determine exactly what the prospective client needs and to form an emotional connection with them. If they can't connect with you emotionally, they won't enroll in your program. Before you meet with your prospective client, outline your key questions in the following ways:

- Ask how they heard of you and what brings them in to see you.
- Ask follow-up questions to each answer they give you about the issue they're struggling with so you can get a sense of the underlying root cause.
- Ask how that issue is affecting them (i.e., what is the financial, emotional, and physical impact of this issue).
- Ask what they've tried up until now to resolve it.
- Avoid the temptation to offer your services too soon. Keep listening and remain unattached to whether they sign up with you.
- Avoid the temptation to tell them how to address the issue. This will amount to free advice that they won't value and won't apply. If you do give free advice, they'll think this is all they need rather than signing up for your service.

You can help them see what the issue is, without telling them how to address it. As a simple example, imagine that your prospective client is describing digestive health issues. You know that the issues are indicative of imbalanced gut flora (this is the what). You also know that this can be addressed with antimicrobial products, probiotics, and dietary changes (this is the how). Do not go into detail about the how (the supplements and dietary changes). This will either overwhelm the prospect, or they will think they can take that advice and try it on their own rather than enrolling in their program. Then they'll go home, make a halfhearted attempt at this regimen, and possibly make the issue worse.

After you help them see what the issue is (without saying how to resolve it), reflect back to them, in their own words, to show that you understand how they feel and how this is impacting them. If applicable, also refer to the prospect's results from a quiz, questionnaire, or lab test as evidence of what the issue is and how it correlates to how they feel. Black and white on paper can be a very powerful visual tool to help your prospect see the picture you're presenting.

If your program is indeed a good fit for the prospect, briefly tell them about it. Don't focus on the features of the program (such as the number of sessions or price). Instead, focus on the benefits and results they can expect to derive from the program. How will they feel as a result of the program? What will their day-to-day life look like? Paint a vivid picture while recalling the language and examples they presented to you earlier.

Provide testimonials from other clients or prospects with whom this prospect can identify. Quote specific statements from those clients. Again, paint a vivid picture.

You may or may not feel comfortable offering a "fast-action" discount if they decide to enroll in that moment rather than taking time to think about it. (Many business coaching programs will recommend that you offer this.) While it is true that incentives to "reward" decisive action can be helpful, if it doesn't align with who you are, don't do it. Always be true to yourself.

If your prospective client does need time to think about it, do agree on a specific day to follow up. Consistent follow-up is always key, regardless of whether you're a dedicated salesperson, a coach, or a healthcare practitioner. Remember that people get busy and overwhelmed. And a confused mind doesn't buy. So present them with a clear offering and agree on a specific time and way to follow up.

Don't be afraid to uncover objections or hesitations if you sense them. While you remain unattached to the outcome, you can use gentle curiosity to uncover the hidden doubts and fears you sense in your prospective client. Use gentle phrases, such as "I'm sensing I haven't answered all your questions. Is there anything else you're wondering about?" or "I get the feeling I didn't do a thorough job explaining the benefits of this program. What else might I have missed?"

Above all, as the coach or practitioner, you are the leader in the conversation. Your questions will create a safe container where the prospective client can share their challenges and how the challenges have affected them emotionally. Your job is not to solve those challenges in that initial conversation; instead, your job is to show them how your program (services) will bring about the outcome and feelings that they desire. As you do so, remain attuned to their emotional state. Help them to feel understood by reflecting back to them using the same words and language they use.

CHAPTER 17: RECAP AND DAILY PRACTICES FOR SALES SUCCESS

Your dreams and desires contain within them the necessary spark to turn any business plan into a reality. If you start with a business plan that is not rooted in your dreams and desires, it will fall flat because it will lack the momentum needed to turn the original thought (goal) into reality. Embrace your dreams and desires, and from there, reverse engineer a practical business plan that specifies the exact strategies to get you to the end goal. Loving consciousness will speed you along in the process, but you still need to have a concrete plan that includes the number of calls you'll make each day, the marketing strategies you'll use, and the number of clients you aim to serve.

To this end, I have three critical exercises for you to complete. To complete these exercises (and access bonus resources), please be sure to download your free HPS Companion Workbook at robintreasure.com/workbook.

Exercise 6: Create Your Heart-Powered Statement:

Your heart-powered statement is a powerful tool to anchor your goals in a concise paragraph that includes your gratitude for the realization of this goal as if it has already been reached. Repeat this statement every day, trusting fully that it will come to pass, even if you don't know exactly how.

To create your statement,

1. Write down your goal.
2. Make sure your goal aligns with your deeper desires.
3. Write how you will serve others in working toward this goal.
4. Express gratitude for the realization of this goal.

I've included a sample heart-powered statement in the HPS Companion Workbook.

Exercise 7: Create Your Business Plan:

Follow the steps in this chapter and in the HPS Companion Workbook to create your business plan. Review your plan at least once per week, and be sure to give yourself a performance review at the end of each quarter. Don't be afraid to identify any areas where you fell short of your plan. Being honest with yourself is the best way to improve and adapt as needed.

Exercise 8: Evaluate Your Alignment:

Just as it is important to review your business plan, which is composed of measurable goals, it is also important to check in with yourself about the less quantifiable but equally vital quality of your sales engagements. I recommend reflecting on your business meetings periodically, and asking yourself:

- Do I love and believe in the products or services I represent?
- Do I enjoy and respect the customers that I serve?
- Do I ask open-ended questions rather than rushing to offer a solution?
- Do I listen carefully, and pay attention to body language, tone of voice, and energy?
- Do I help my customers to feel understood and less overwhelmed?
- Do I present my offering only once I've understood the true need, and do I make sure the offering meets that need?
- Do I follow through on deliverables?
- Do I trust that loving consciousness has my back, so I'm not coming from a place of scarcity in my meetings?
- Do I celebrate my wins and express gratitude for prosperity?

If the answer to any of the above questions is no, this isn't a failure! Practice compassionate questioning with yourself. For any no answers, ask yourself:

- What is missing here?
- What would it take to get me to answer yes to this question?
- Who do I know—or what resource is there—to help me turn this answer into a yes?

PART 4:

THRIVE THROUGH CRISIS

AND AVOID COMMON PITFALLS

CHAPTER 18: CRISIS IS OPPORTUNITY

Inevitably, we all experience some form of crisis at various points in our lives. Sometimes the crisis is death or loss, sometimes it's financial, sometimes it's existential . . . and sometimes it's all of the above. As it happens, I've written this book during the COVID-19 pandemic. For many of us, this has been a crisis of a magnitude we've never witnessed before. We have been forced to adapt how we work, socialize, and participate in the economy. The collective fear of an economic disaster and public health crisis created a whole new world overnight.

With this pandemic, we have a macrocosmic crisis, along with the microcosmic crisis that each of us has faced to different degrees. Each of us is being forced to evolve and grow. Each of us is being offered an opportunity to adapt and to draw on resources within us that we didn't know we had. The immediacy and inescapability of the pandemic have squeezed us into a collective birth canal, compelling us to transform into our "other selves," where we can achieve growth and success—not in spite of but because of—the crisis we face.

The pandemic has affected people to different degrees in the US, depending on their race and economic status. The pandemic itself has exacerbated racial and economic inequalities in this country. The intersection of a public health crisis, economic disaster, manifestations of systemic racism, and the terrifying rifts in political leadership are enough to make anyone wonder if loving consciousness actually exists.

Even when the present can seem dark and rife with turmoil, we have to recognize that loving consciousness is always with us, always guiding us to something better. In fact, the darkest hours are often right before the dawn. Because crisis holds the seeds of transformation and change, we may be on the brink of marvelous transformation. This begins with allowing ourselves to see things differently. It begins with allowing for the possibility that opportunity can be found in the most challenging moments.

Just as the COVID-19 pandemic has highlighted the need for social and economic justice in the US, it has also heightened the specific needs of everyday businesses and consumers. Herein lies the opportunity for your sales career. As new needs and problems arise, can you show up with a solution? You may have to adapt your message, product, or service to suit the needs that have arisen from the pandemic, but by doing so, you reap the benefits of increased sales, personal growth, and a greater sense of resilience and adaptability. Even more importantly, you can shine your light to help share love and hope with those who need it.

Adapting to a crisis

Just as surrender is the first step to dropping into your heart, surrender is the first step in adapting to a crisis. Resistance will only drain your energy—precious energy that you need in the time of a crisis. Loving consciousness has brought this crisis for a reason. What is it here to teach you? How can you emerge from this as a stronger, wiser, more resilient person who can hold space for deep joy and deep sorrow too? In what ways will your creativity and adaptability bring about the success you desire?

Let's take the pandemic as an example. How can we adapt to this crisis? It can affect how we conduct our business—and especially the economy at large. Yet because of this pandemic, women in sales are emerging with great strength and success. Why? Because more than ever before, the world needs compassion, empathy, and connection, and sales is an opportunity to share these values in our daily work because sales is all about relationships.

When social distancing forced us to meet with customers from our homes over Zoom rather than in doctors' offices, many of my colleagues and I were actually able to deepen our customer relationships by getting a glimpse into one another's personal lives. Taking the time to ask a customer how the pandemic has affected their practice and asking thoughtful follow-up questions to understand exactly what they needed provided many opportunities to be of even greater value to our clients than ever before.

For example, two of my colleagues—Evelyne and Stephanie—began holding regular "coffee meetings" over Zoom with a group of their clients after the pandemic started. As the conversations unfolded, it became clear that many of their clients needed help with technical questions related to transforming their businesses online. Evelyne and Stephanie arranged to have a guest expert speak to that group of clients to help address their questions. The topic had nothing to do with immediate sales for Evelyne and Stephanie, but their brilliant resourcefulness helped to build long-lasting relationships with their clients based on value and appreciation, and it helped their clients to succeed in their businesses. Here is what one client of theirs said about the coffee meetings:

> *I'm so impressed by the initiative Evelyne and Stephanie took right out of the gate to create a virtual space to connect during the pandemic. Within a short amount of time, they had a dedicated group of wellness professionals eager to meet up every week. Now, many months on, their practitioner community is still thriving. The weekly Zoom calls have featured an organic blend of guest speakers, success/struggle shares, accountability support, product training, and resource sharing. I appreciate the creativity, effort and dedication these women have to nurture their tribe. For me, it's been a bright spot in these challenging and mostly isolated times.*

Incredible opportunities can come about during a crisis. Another colleague of mine recently made one of the largest sales in his career—exponentially larger than any sale he had made up until then—because one of his clients decided to sell his medical practice due to the economic pressure brought on by the pandemic. The doctor used the money from the sale to create his own brand of customized supplement packets that he designed in consultation with my colleague. Essentially, the doctor adapted and turned the pandemic into an opportunity to evolve into his entrepreneurial self by launching an online resale business that would significantly benefit the health of his online customers. The doctor's opening order of the customized packets was ten times the size of the largest order my colleague had received up until then.

Change is inevitable

You may have heard it said that the only constant in life is change. In other words, nothing is permanent. Rather than resisting change, or clutching on to happy moments hoping they won't end, we can achieve more happiness in sales—and in life—by recognizing the impermanence of it all. Things will change. They always do—both the good and the bad. The question is, how will we change and adapt with it?

What can make it all bearable, in times of uncertainty, is the knowing that nothing is permanent. Nothing. Not the pandemic. Not a recession. Not a downturn in sales. It will all change, sooner or later. By the same token, joy, prosperity, and good luck are also impermanent.

The peace is in the stillness deep within. The stillness that is unshakable, because it's your core. It's that part of your being that is directly connected to loving consciousness. It's your connection to a deeper truth, which frees you from having to fix the present disaster or figure out how to hold onto joy forever.

The pandemic has made it painfully clear that we never really know what will happen, ever, with anything. Normally we hold on to the illusion that we're in control and can foresee the outcome. But the key to riding the wave of any crisis, including a downturn in sales, is to become comfortable with the not-knowing and allow yourself to grow and transform by remaining anchored to loving consciousness.

Essentially, the key is accepting the change. Accepting change comes back to energy. As mentioned, energy plays a huge role in the success of your sales. If you're resisting what is, or striving from a place of desperation, that desperation will leak into your sales like seeping floodwaters. The energy of resistance or desperation will derail even the best strategies and the hardest work. Energy is everything. And it's the energy—not the circumstances—that determines success in sales.

Once you accept the impermanence of things and the not-knowing, you experience a great freedom that gives you the confidence to do things like cold call a prospective client, ask for a sale, or ask for a referral. Surrendering and accepting impermanence allow you to transform the weighty "sales process" into a game, where you get to experiment and observe without attachment. Your best skills are allowed to come out to play, without having to answer to any big expectations.

Fear and growth

By contrast, the energy of fear will weigh you down. Fear is the quickest way to stifle your playfulness and trip up your attempts to close a deal. Not only does fear bring a weighty attachment to the outcome but it also becomes a self-fulfilling prophecy that the outcome will equate to failure. Fear is natural, and it reflects our strong instinct for self-preservation. Yet fear is what happens when we forget that we are connected to loving consciousness. We may not be able to see the light at the end of the tunnel. We may have no idea what lies ahead in the nebulous, murky waters before us. But if we can remain connected to loving consciousness (through surrendering and connecting to our intuition), we will emerge as beings that are more resilient, more successful, and more joyful than ever before.

We all face fears, no matter what industry or career track we're in. (I will address specific types of fear shortly.) For now, suffice it to say that overcoming your fears and surmounting challenges is exactly what will allow you to experience deep personal growth and amaze yourself with what you can achieve.

For this reason, sales is one of the greatest platforms for personal growth. This is a career track that can present you with the greatest challenges you could have ever imagined, especially in times of crisis. Yet with crisis comes the greatest opportunity for growth, and in sales, you are on the leading edge of change and growth.

Your greatest personal growth may happen at the same time that you experience a devastating drop in sales. If we measured the success of your sales based on the old metrics of strictly looking at positive or negative numbers, you might consider yourself a failure at these times. But that old paradigm is fading out. The evolution of sales employs much more inclusive measurements of success beyond simple dollar signs and conventional growth metrics. In fact, the "failure" of a drastic drop in sales will often prompt your greatest breakthroughs in personal growth and sales techniques—as long as you focus on the right areas.

Allow me to share a story to illustrate what I mean. In March 2020, when the COVID-19 pandemic was underway and the shelter-in-place directives were instituted, sales in my industry actually ballooned because of the surge in demand for supplements to support the immune system. Even though we could no longer meet with customers face-to-face, the demand for our products surged. We simply had to keep up and respond to the influx of orders and questions from our clients each day. My sales in March 2020 were 111 percent above the sales from March 2019. Is that when I experienced great personal growth? No. Even though I was enormously grateful to be in an industry that was prospering while helping people, I wasn't being stretched to grow in that moment.

The growth happened the following month, in April 2020, when my sales suddenly took a nosedive. This happened partly because customers had already "stocked up" the month before and partly because of the fear of economic collapse that pervaded everyone's minds. Did I take these factors into stride and reassure myself that I was still a success in the bigger picture? Not immediately. I will be honest with you: at first I was overcome with thoughts such as

"I'm a failure who has just gotten lucky up till now."

"I'm not nearly as innovative and polished as my colleagues."

"I feel like I've turned over every stone and nothing is working this month."

Sound familiar? In those low moments, do you feel like you're going through the greatest personal growth? I sure didn't.

So when did my growth actually take place? The growth happened when I dropped back down into my heart and reminded myself that I was connected to loving consciousness. The growth happened when I shifted out of self-pity and doubt, and I asked myself, "What can I learn in this moment?" That one question enabled me to look beyond my temporary obstacles. It helped me to learn from my colleagues rather than comparing myself to them. (Comparing is despairing, as they say.)

I looked at the innovative ways my colleagues were joining forces and presenting webinars to their customers, and I was inspired to do the same. I got back in touch with my intuition—and said goodbye to those nagging questions of self-doubt. I was immediately guided to reach out to the right customers at the right time. I looked beyond what I had already tried without success and, instead, recognized the infinite opportunities for providing value to my customers. I implemented clear action plans on paper and stuck to them rather than getting distracted and overwhelmed.

In taking these steps, I was once again heart-powered. I had shifted my mindset back to infinite possibility. By the very next month, my sales were up by 41 percent over the same month last year. And I was able to set and achieve an ambitious goal of enrolling five customers into a special educational program with minimal effort.

The art of getting over yourself

The underlying theme behind the actions that I took to get out of despair and back into a position of success was that I got over myself. I moved beyond the small-mindedness of doubting myself and comparing myself to others. Instead, I adopted a perspective of "What can I learn here? How can I collaborate with others? How can I provide value to my clients?"

It's downright hard to ride the waves of sales cycles. If you had a great month last month, it's natural to experience a dip in sales the following month. When your growth rate compares your sales this month versus your sales in the same month last year, you're in direct competition with yourself. It may be deflating to realize that your great performance last year will make you struggle this year to beat those high numbers. Then compound those normal challenges with something like the COVID pandemic, and you might just have a recipe for despair.

When the economy flounders, it's easy to get trapped into anxiety-provoking fears of how you will be able to survive, let alone continue a strong growth rate in sales. This is where surrendering comes in. Trust that you will be okay, no matter what. Surrender to where loving consciousness wants to take you, even if it means a temporary contraction in your sales or a shift in your career.

Does surrendering mean you give up on any hope of success in your sales career? No way! Surrendering is empowering. When you stop your mental and emotional resistance, you free up your energy so it can be channeled in a much more positive direction.

When you surrender and connect to something larger than yourself, you experience great personal growth, which then leads to the greatest growth in your sales—in the most authentic, organic way possible. Learning not to be affected by your sales numbers will most likely be an ongoing challenge. Yet it's the difficult moments of "failure" that compel you to flex your muscles, get over yourself, and evolve into more of who you really are. In this way, you can contribute something much larger than yourself in collaboration with others. This will result in the most sustainable and authentic sales growth possible.

CHAPTER 19: COMMON PITFALL #1: FEAR

Based on observations of myself and conversations with many women in sales over the years, I would say the number one challenge or pitfall that we face is fear: fear of being pushy, fear of being salesy, and fear of being rejected. What will limit or impede your success is not actually being pushy or being rejected . . . it's fear! Fear is the obstacle that will put a spoke in your wheel and hamper your best-intentioned efforts. As Franklin D. Roosevelt said, "The only thing we have to fear is fear itself."

Dealing with fear

Can we snap our fingers and make fear disappear? No. But one simple thing you can do is mentally walk yourself through a scenario where you are feeling fear. Let's say you're procrastinating on calling a prospect because you're afraid of rejection.

Ask, what's the worst that can happen? They'll hang up on you? Will that destroy you? No. If they hang up on you, it just might make you unhappy for a half hour. What is the likelihood that they'll hang up on you? Probably minimal. What if, instead, the phone call goes well, and you make a great connection with the prospect? Perhaps you set up a meeting with them? Think of all the potential benefits that could arise from making that one phone call, such as a nice big order, followed by many more big orders and referrals. But none of that will happen if you let fear get the best of you and you don't make the phone call.

Brendon Burchard has a chapter dedicated to fear and courage in his book *High Performance Habits*. He writes, "Courage is not fearlessness; it is taking action and persisting despite that fear." If you wait until your fear dissipates, you will never take action. Feel the fear and do it anyway.

In my interview with Camila Arri-Nudo, I asked her what she has done to overcome her fears. "Make more calls?" she chuckled. After describing a time when a prospect did hang up on her, she said, "It's about keeping things in perspective and reminding yourself of all the other prospects and opportunities that are out there and not focusing on that one bit of rejection."

When you do experience rejection, relish it as an opportunity to learn what you could do better next time. Most likely there are far more prospects and opportunities than you could ever actually serve. So try to view those instances of rejection as playground lessons: you had an opportunity to interact with someone—like kids on a playground—and you got to learn more about yourself, so you could become stronger and more confident in the future. Even try to feel gratitude toward that prospect who rejected you, for giving you the opportunity to learn and grow.

I'd be willing to bet that outright rejection happens to you quite rarely. Instead, it's the fear of rejection that trips you up. You don't need to suppress the fear. Allow yourself to feel it, and let it actually move through you so it doesn't get stuck. Use your somatic intelligence to feel how the fear shows up in your body, so you can acknowledge it and release it.

To help you cope with fear, the biggest tool in your arsenal is being aware of your connection to loving consciousness. When you can trust that a benevolent force far greater than you is guiding you toward your highest good, even if there are playground moments of rejection and failure, you will be far more empowered in any situation. You can feel the fear and know that, ultimately, you will enjoy success because you are being guided to it by loving consciousness.

Courage isn't the opposite of fear. Courage means taking action from the heart despite the fear. The root of the word "courage" is the Latin word for heart: *cor*. (The French word for heart is *cœur*). In the face of any adversity or challenge, surrender and connect to your heart. In the face of fear, surrendering means accepting the existence of any struggle and moving forward anyway. As Brendon Burchard writes:

The difficulties in life that you can't avoid? Engage them wholeheartedly. Even when you feel overwhelmed, choose to go for a walk, focus on your breath, and consider the problem rather than avoid it. Look the problem in the eye and ask, "What is the next right action for me to take right now?" If you aren't yet ready to take that action, plan. Study. Prepare yourself for when the fog lifts and you are called to lead.

Note that Brendon Burchard italicized the phrase "engage them wholeheartedly." Courage is found in your heart. Courage is found when you stop resisting the struggle or challenge, and instead, embrace it as a part of the journey. Burchard also writes, "By meeting the conflicts and difficulties and outright messes of life straight on, willingly, we dismantle the walls of fear, brick by brick."

The key is to go with it. Go with the flow. And feel the feelings, including the fear. Suppressing fear will only create dissonance, and it will dilute your energy. Feel the fear, but don't let it keep you from taking action.

If you let fear take over, it will disconnect you from loving consciousness. If that happens, no worries! All you have to do is reconnect by following the steps back to your heart: surrender (which includes acknowledging and feeling the fear), get into your body (which helps you to be in the present rather than playing into fearful thoughts of rejection or failure), feel into your heart (the root of courage), and activate your intuition (which is your portal to loving consciousness). This process can take just a few minutes, and it will help you to reset and receive the guidance you need to carry out your work.

Don't lose sight of your mission. In some form or another, your mission will be to serve your customer for their highest good. If you represent a product or service that you know will benefit the customer, and if you let fear prevent you from making contact with them, you have departed from your mission.

Also take heed of a more insidious fear: the fear of being truly yourself. Are you holding back from:

- Fully expressing your authentic self?
- Fully owning your achievements?
- Fully and unabashedly feeling your heartfelt power?

Generally speaking, we tend to prioritize humility over authenticity. We want to avoid stepping on anyone's toes, or overshadowing others, or taking up too much space. It is all well and good to remain humble and respectful of others, but if you are living authentically from the heart, you cannot overshadow others. The authentic power that comes from your heart will allow you to bring more good into the world. In doing so, you will empower others to do the same. As Burchard writes:

I've seen a lot of people from all over the world martyr themselves under the guise of a poorly conceived "humility." But there's nothing humble in saying, "I'd better not shine, because the timid souls around me couldn't handle it." Please.

Shine your light! Be fully you. The joy you will feel in living authentically and allowing yourself to be heart-powered is contagious! Your prospects and customers will feel it. They will be drawn to this energy far more than you realize. Far more than they realize. Don't let the fear of being seen hold you back. The light from your heart can only bring more good to a world that desperately needs it.

Take the fear out of cold calling

In sales, cold calling is inevitably what sparks the most fear. Even many seasoned sales professionals still dread cold calling, because the underlying fear is that you're setting yourself up for rejection. After all, it is a lot easier to return to customers who know you and like you than to approach new leads who might give you the cold shoulder or dismiss you before you can get a word in edgewise. Paradoxically, you know that if you don't make cold calls, your business could dry up.

What to say

Showing up to your cold call with positive, confident energy is critical. And knowing what to say and how to say it in the first twenty seconds of your cold call will determine the entire outcome of the engagement.

Come up with a concise and specific opening statement that includes:

- your purpose
- the value you bring

- your request
- the amount of time your request involves

For example, if you are cold calling an acupuncturist's office, you could approach the front desk with the following opening statement, "Hi, my name is Jane, and I'm with [company name]. We have a nutritional supplement that can reduce pain and inflammation as effectively as over-the-counter pain meds, but without the side effects (the value you bring). I'd like to request five minutes with [acupuncturist's name] to see if this would be a fit for her patients in chronic pain (purpose). What would be the best way to meet with her so I'm not interrupting her patient schedule?" (request).

With this opening statement, you've:

- painted a quick picture of the value you can bring to their patient base
- described a specific product to suit their needs, because you qualified the prospect beforehand
- requested a specific amount of time
- preempted the most common brush-off you get, which is that "the doctor is busy seeing patients"
- asked an open-ended question in order to empower the front desk person to recommend the best way to proceed

What happens after your pitch

On your first attempt, the front desk person may ask you to "just leave some information." This is not a dead-end rejection. Do comply with their request, but use it as an opportunity to ask for their insight into what will best serve the doctor—if the front desk person appears unrushed. For example, you could say, "Sure, I'd be happy to leave some information. I just want to be sure I'm not cluttering your desk unnecessarily. What would you say is the most important type of information to provide for [acupuncturist's name] as she considers products for pain?" In doing so, you are showing the front desk person that you value their perspective and insight. The relationship you establish with the front desk person is just as important as the relationship with the ultimate decision maker.

But if the front desk person appears rushed when they ask you to leave some information, simply reply with, "Of course. Here is some information on the product I mentioned. When would be a good time for me to follow up with you?" Commit to following up with them at that time.

Earlier, we reviewed the importance of starting with impactful questions and listening carefully to the answers. Cold calling is different. With cold calling, you've qualified your prospect so you know a bit about them, but they have no idea who you are. You can't call or walk into their office, state your name, and ask them if they have five minutes. Five minutes for what? They will wonder. Remember, as a general rule, people are busy and overwhelmed. It's just as important to concisely state the value you bring, as it is to ask for a specific amount of their time.

It's also far more effective to mention a specific product or a specific problem you solve rather than introducing yourself in broad strokes. Put yourself in the shoes of an acupuncturist who has patients in chronic pain. What would catch your attention more: the mention of a specific product for pain and how it compares to other remedies for pain on the market, or a broad statement like "I'm with a company that makes nutritional supplements"?

While you probably won't get a meeting on the spot, if you present your offering with confidence, it can lead to a solid next step forward: a meeting on the calendar or, at least, making a connection with the front desk person so you can determine when to follow up with them. You may even need to make several attempts before you make any progress. Remember that consistent follow-up is key.

Dispelling the fear of cold calling

Two critical elements can help you dispel your fear:

- Practice (i.e., repetition). Just do it. Again and again and again. Set a daily goal for how many cold calls you will make. With each new prospect that you cold call, it will get easier and easier. You don't have full control over how many deals you close today, but you do have full control over how many cold calls you make.

- Approach each cold call with the intention to provide value to your prospect. This intention, and your positive energy, will ensure that you show up in the best possible way, with a specific offer of value.

Many of my most cherished clients were once unknown prospects whom I cold called. Many of them required multiple cold calls before we sat down to a meeting, and sometimes multiple meetings were needed before an order was placed. Yet later they made it clear how much they appreciated my consistent follow-up and the value I brought to the meetings. They were aware of the positive energy and positive intentions I brought.

One such client is Maryam Fortani, MD. When she learned I was writing this book, she wrote me:

I remember the very first day I met you in my office. I felt positive energy from you and I recognized that you are one of those people on this planet that are working for the common good. I knew that you work with your heart and have been blessed with an intuition that helps you to navigate through the day by giving everyone what is needed at that moment. For me, your "random" sales visits to my office were accompanied by synchronistic experiences to the point that I would tell myself, "Today Robin will show up and help me with the question I had yesterday in my mind," and you would show up.

Dr. Fortani's remarks were a powerful affirmation of my efforts, especially since I had to make multiple attempts to meet with her in the beginning. But over time, I was able to help her with several different questions and challenges she had in her practice. We built a solid business relationship based on this trust and value. Imagine if I hadn't ever built up the courage to walk into her office. Imagine if I had been put off the first time her front desk person told me she was busy with patients.

Which prospects need the value you offer, right now? If you let your fear of rejection keep you from picking up the phone or walking into that office, what have you gained from playing it safe? On the flipside, what is your prospect missing out on if your fear of rejection prevents you from approaching them? Shift your attention away from your fears and, instead, focus on the value you can provide to your prospects. With time, and with enough cold calls, you will begin to own the incredible value you have to offer.

CHAPTER 20: COMMON PITFALL #2:

SHINY OBJECTS AND OVERWHELM

The next most common pitfall is distraction. You could also call it "shiny object syndrome." Each day you have countless options of where to devote your time and attention: cultivating and growing existing accounts, prospecting for new accounts, following up with customers on pending orders and questions, and using your various tools to grow your business. With the multitude of actions to choose from, and all the distractions around us, it's very easy to get distracted and overwhelmed.

Avoiding shiny object syndrome

To avoid shiny object syndrome, try the tips below.

Consistent customer outreach is the key to success

If you see great potential in a prospect, keep following up with them. It may take multiple attempts and meetings before you get their business. Meanwhile, dozens of other shiny objects (prospects) may catch your eye, but don't let those other prospects prevent you from consistently following up with the prospects who have the most potential.

I've had countless examples of great prospects who took quite a bit of consistent touchpoints before I made a sale, and along the way, countless other opportunities could have distracted me from consistently following up.

I remember stopping in at one particular chiropractor's office as a cold call. I had no relationship with the chiropractor, but I could see how well-suited our products were to her practice. My first two attempts at the office were met with mild interest from the staff, but they said the chiropractor already had all the products she needed. Even though those first two attempts didn't result in a meeting with the head chiropractor, I gathered enough information to learn that the chiropractor had a big focus on digestive health with her patients. So the third time I stopped in, I informed them of a diagnostic test that wasn't a direct product I represented, but it was a valuable resource to offer practitioners. Fortunately, that offer piqued the interest of the staff member, who helped me get a meeting on the calendar with the chiropractor for the following week. Within a month, the chiropractor was ordering about $400 in product per month, and within eighteen months, she was consistently ordering at least $11,000 in product per month.

If I had given up after two attempts and moved on to a "shinier object," I would have missed out on building what has become an amazing collaborative partnership with that chiropractor.

In my interview with Camila Arri-Nudo, she describes the importance of being "pleasantly persistent": "When you are persistent and consistent in your follow-up, and when you use emotional intelligence to appropriately and respectfully respond to your prospect's cues, you will be able to learn what your prospect needs. You can then present them with a solution that will build a relationship based on value and mutual trust."

Pick two tools to build your business

Be consistent not only in your interactions with customers but also in the tools that you implement to build your business. Don't try to use all the tools. While you can try various ones out and see what works for you, once you know what works, just pick two and stick with them.

Maybe you've thought about sending newsletters to your customers. This is something I would highly recommend, but only if you love to write! That may seem obvious, but I've seen lots of entrepreneurs engage in activities they don't love, only because those activities have worked for other people. It won't work if you don't love it. And it won't work if you don't do it consistently. If you do love writing, pick a frequency for your newsletter that feels feasible to you (such as once per week or once per month), and then stick to it! When you send out your first couple of newsletters, you may hear crickets. Not to worry! Keep at it if you enjoy the process and if you have valuable content to share with your customers. Over time, it will be a great way for you to reach many more people than you would be able to individually on any given day.

I love the process of writing a weekly newsletter, and I attribute a lot of my sales growth to how it has enabled me to reach more customers and leads. I try to keep it as content-rich as possible. Even when it is an outright promotion of a particular product, I focus on the value it can bring my readers. I include special promotions and offers, usually as a secondary item to the main content. Other times my newsletters are more personal, and occasionally, I'll include pictures from a vacation or conference. This has enabled me to build and maintain relationships with my customers and extend my reach. The consistency of the newsletter and the value and personal touch help to cultivate the trust my clients have in me.

Other sales professionals are great with social media. They're consistent about posting great content in bite-sized pieces, so they remain top of mind with their audience. A few random posts here and there won't get you anywhere, but if you post regularly, and if you respond and adapt your content based on the comments and feedback you get from your audience, social media becomes an amazing tool to help you grow your business.

One more tool I have used in my business is to host monthly webinars with guest speakers. This does require a fair amount of work, but it's an amazing way to deliver in-depth content to many of your customers all at once. You don't need to create all that content from scratch! Host a guest speaker who already has that content created—maybe even one of your customers. This way, you can deepen your relationships, reach many more customers, and even start building a network or community by providing a common forum where professionals or consumers can connect with one another.

As you decide what to pick, keep in mind that it should be something you love doing and can do consistently. Along the way, you will hear of plenty of other great methods to build your business. These will be the shiny objects that could distract you from the tools you originally committed to. You've picked a lane—stay in it! Only abandon those tools if after an earnest, consistent use of them you don't see the results you're looking for. Consistency doesn't mean you need to remain blindly committed to something that isn't working. But first, give them a fair shot in order to determine if a tool will get you the results you want.

Don't hide behind busywork

One more distraction is allowing busywork and service-related activities to take you away from the goal of growing your sales. Whoa! You might say, "Didn't you say earlier that service is what it's all about?!" Yes, sales is primarily about service, even if it doesn't immediately result in a sale. But just be sure to stay engaged in meaningful actions with prospects and customers that you've qualified. Don't devote time to smaller tasks or customers with no potential as a way of avoiding cold calls. Don't let busywork pull you away from reaching out to an account that hasn't placed an order in a while. We can easily fall into the trap of using busywork to shield us from stepping outside of our comfort zone.

Be sure to only commit to acts of service and administrative work if they are necessary and called for. Only you can determine where that line is drawn. If you go beyond that line, stop and ask yourself what you might be avoiding.

Getting out of overwhelm

Whereas shiny object syndrome can keep you hopping from one prospect to the next, overwhelm can leave you feeling helpless and paralyzed. If you're expected to take a new training program every week, attend countless meetings, keep up with existing accounts, find new accounts, and meet your sales quota, you might find yourself crippled by these external pressures. You probably feel that you don't have enough hours in a day to keep up with everything you should be doing. I get it. Overwhelm is something I deal with regularly.

To get out of overwhelm, connect back to your heart. Overwhelm happens in your mind, not your heart. Overwhelm is compounded by the racing thoughts of what you should be doing and how impossible it is to do it all. In these moments, take just five minutes to shift your mindset.

- Surrender. Release the thoughts of what you should be doing or how unbearable the situation is.
- Bring your awareness to the physical area of your heart.
- Think of something you love, something you are grateful for.
- Spend as much time as you want activating these feelings of love and gratitude.
- Ask your intuition, "What is my next best step?" This will be your most impactful action, not the myriad of activities that don't matter in the grander scheme of your business and life. Focus on that one action. Ignore all the rest, until it is time to decide again on your next best step.

CHAPTER 21: COMMON PITFALL #3:

IMPOSTER SYNDROME

It's not uncommon for women to blame themselves when things go sideways, and to chalk it up to luck when things go well. Imposter syndrome is real. It can be defined as the inability to believe that one's success is deserved or has been legitimately achieved as a result of one's own efforts or skills.

In college, I was a *summa cum laude* student, and I was proud of that, but a part of me felt like an imposter because I majored in European cultural studies. I secretly cringed with the thought that European cultural studies wasn't a "real" major, and if I had majored in something "legitimate," like science or math, I would've had terrible grades. So with my *summa cum laude* status, I felt like a fraud. But if I ever got a disappointing grade on an exam or paper, I was quick to blame myself for not studying harder, for not being smarter.

Fast forward twenty-five years to the present, where many times I've experienced sales growth of 30–60 percent, and yet underneath my pride and satisfaction lies a slight but persistent thought that I've just gotten lucky all this time. A nagging question and negative thoughts linger in my mind: When will they find out that I'm not really a salesperson? I'm an imposter. A fraud. And now I'm writing a book about sales! Who am I to write a book on sales? I hardly know what I'm doing.

Can you relate to any of this? I imagine you can, and that's actually one of the reasons why I am writing this book. I've come to accept that this is a normal feeling, especially amongst high-achieving women. If we don't shed enough light on the imposter syndrome, it festers underneath the surface instead.

The truth is, we're all learning as we go, and we never feel like a complete expert at anything. Parenting is the best example of this. The only training we get is being raised by imperfect parents. Then we grow up, have a child of our own, and we figure it out as we go. As soon as we get a handle on one issue (such as how to get the baby to sleep through the night), the next issue comes up (like the terrible twos), and we're back to being a rookie again. As a mom, I feel like a complete imposter, and when I have proud moments of recognizing that my daughter is a healthy, happy, well-adjusted kid, I marvel at how it has happened. I don't feel like I can take any credit for it.

Overcoming imposter syndrome

So, you could say that the antidote to imposter syndrome is to list all the reasons why you're good, and why you deserve the recognition you've gotten. In other words, you can use logic and evidence to counter the self-doubt that comes with the imposter syndrome. This can be helpful, and it's certainly important to own and celebrate your strengths and skills.

On the other hand, countering your self-doubt with evidence and reason misses the deeper truth: none of your success, and none of your failure, is truly yours anyway. Loving consciousness is continuously co-creating your world with you. You do have your gifts and talents, but it's ultimately your connection to loving consciousness that will bring about fortuitous events, serendipitous meetings, big wins, and small steps forward. All of it is a manifestation of the good fortune that loving consciousness wants to bring you, if only you connect to it and allow it. You're never an imposter if you do what you do with love and passion. When you have a winning streak and dismiss it by saying, "I just got lucky," you're denying and dishonoring the magnificent work of loving consciousness, and your own connection to it.

Even temporary roadblocks and "failures" can be the work of loving consciousness using those hurdles to guide you in a different direction. Rather than blaming yourself for that failure (as high achievers are apt to do), you can take solace in knowing that it was part of what loving consciousness wanted to for you, for reasons that have yet to be revealed.

Your success is not really your success, and your failure is not really your failure. This statement can be extremely liberating if you really take it to heart. Does this mean you take no ownership for making mistakes? Not at all! Does this mean you don't get any credit for making a big sale or closing a big new client? Not at all! It's extremely important to take personal responsibility for what you can control and to take pride in your hard work and accomplishments.

Yet the events that transpire as a result of your actions, gifts, talents, decisions, and even misgivings are all determined by loving consciousness. This means you can release attachment to any outcome—whether it's a success or a failure. The emotional attachment to success and failure—and how you allow it to define you—is what creates anguish, including the self-doubt of feeling like an imposter. If you allow your emotional attachment to take over, you will be cut off from your connection to loving consciousness.

As the wise spiritual adviser Erin Reese says, "Success and failure are only perception. Everything is always in perfect alignment. Relax into it."

And yet, it's only natural to seek success in your sales career. Attachment is something I experience regularly, but then I remind myself to let go. If I let go of attachment, I can let go of the tortuous stories that come with claiming the "success" and "failure" as being "mine." There's something much bigger at play in your sales career. It's not all about you. You're co-creating with loving consciousness. This means you can avoid the trappings of clinging too tightly to your success. You don't have to wonder if you deserve your wins, nor do you need to blame yourself for your losses.

Reframe your success as gratitude

While it's important to celebrate your successes, you should do so from a place of gratitude. Gratitude is the best practice of all, and it will bring more abundance, and more success, without limitation. Loving consciousness is ultimately what brought you that success, so you can celebrate the success as a co-creation with it. When you reframe your success in this way, the imposter syndrome naturally falls away.

Let's say you just won an award for top sales growth in your company. Outwardly, you're thrilled, but you're secretly plagued with self-doubt, feeling like you don't really deserve the award or you just "got lucky." If you take a moment to recognize the role that loving consciousness played in your success, it validates your thought that the success wasn't really yours. Yet the reframe shifts your attention away from your-self (your ego) and into a state of appreciation for the benev-olent power of loving consciousness. It immediately removes the emotional attachment that would have led you to dismiss your success as pure luck.

There is so much suffering in letting success or failure de-fine you. Emotional attachment to success means that as soon as the success slips away, you're no longer the "success" you identified with. And letting failure define you is pure suffer-ing, for obvious reasons.

It's a wonderful feeling of freedom when you embrace the idea that your success is not really your success, and your failure is not really your failure. When you stop fretting over whether you are an imposter, or what your success or failure means about you, your energy is freed up to use your gifts and talents to the best of your ability. Most of all, shift your attention away from your self-doubt, and instead, focus on how you can serve your clients and bring them value. It's not about you. It's about how you can show up for others.

Have I completely released attachment to success and failure? Nope. But I'm well aware of the deep contrast between the freedom I feel when I release attachment to success and failure, and the angst I feel when I revert to my old pattern of letting these things define me. I'm sharing this with you precisely because I'm not a master, and I experience the contrast of these states frequently.

You may be wondering why I've written an entire book on how to achieve success in sales if I'm now telling you that the success isn't really yours. There's a bit of a paradox here, to be fair, especially in the statement that "success and failure are only perception." Does this mean we should just give up on trying to win the sale or reach our goals? Not at all! We can experience desire, set goals, work hard to achieve those goals, engage our gifts and talents, and delight in the "win" of achieving those goals—all while remaining aware that none of it is purely determined by our own doing. By surrendering your emotional attachment to the outcome, while joining forces with the awe-inspiring, benevolent loving consciousness, your path to success will be accelerated like a gentle but fast-flowing river. You will be able to enjoy prosperity, ease, and joy, all while being of service to others.

CHAPTER 22: RECAP AND DAILY PRACTICES FOR NAVIGATING CRISIS AND AVOIDING COMMON PITFALLS

A s you employ the Heart-Powered Sales Method, you will still find yourself in moments of crisis, and you may succumb to common pitfalls. As imperfect humans, it is natural to have these moments. But remember to:

- Surrender and drop the resistance, because resistance only drains your energy.
- Ask yourself what the crisis is here to teach you.
- Engage in possibility thinking.
- Tap into the incredible strength you have as a woman to flex and adapt to the changing circumstances around you.

- Find ways to connect to your customers and loved ones with compassion and empathy. Remember that nothing is permanent.
- Connect to something larger than yourself: loving consciousness.
- Allow yourself to feel fear, but don't let it prevent you from taking action.
- Keep your attention and focus on your mission and purpose, and on your connection to loving consciousness.
- Avoid distraction (see practice steps below).
- Notice if and when you experience imposter syndrome (see practice steps below).

To avoid distraction, identify a few key strategies for reaching out to prospects and growing your existing accounts. Then commit to those actions by dedicating regular time to them in your calendar. Ignore any shiny objects that might detract from the time and energy you dedicate to the key strategies you've identified.

As you progress through your career, notice if and when you experience imposter syndrome. Remind yourself that your success is never entirely your own, nor are your failures. Continue to celebrate your wins, and take personal responsibility for shortcomings, but remember that you're always co-creating with loving consciousness.

SUMMARY

As we navigate our sales careers and daily lives, it all starts within our hearts, and in the energy with which we show up each day.

We may each be navigating our individual paths, but we don't have to go it alone. We all have a limitless wealth of guidance available and immediately accessible to us if we only remove the barriers standing in the way and connect to that guidance through our intuition.

Though you have loving consciousness to guide you, you still must take decisive action, never waiting passively for fortune to show up. Yet the action we take is much more effective and strategically defined when we're first connected to loving consciousness.

One of the most important actions we can take is to engage in sales meetings with our customers in a consultative sales approach that is customer-centric and rooted in emotional intelligence. Enormous opportunities open up when you are unencumbered by fear or personal motives and when you are completely present for your customer. By clearly defining your goals and reviewing them regularly, while releasing attachment to how they manifest, you can better focus on the highest good of the customer. Ultimately this brings about greater sales growth for you, along with greater benefit to your customers.

ACKNOWLEDGMENTS

Thank you to the early supporters of this book: Ann Affinito, Amanda Baldwin, Rebekah Bastian, Sabrina Bayles, Marie Bowser, Laura Capuzzi, Kevin Cardenas, Nathan Cheong, Tamar Cohen, Danica D'Emilio, Marlo Dalby, Amy Day, Lyse de Bourguignon, Jonathan DeYoe, Michelle Dwyer, Nycole Evans Hammond, Lorie Gehrke, Christina Gunn, Kelly Hall, Mimi Hart, Ashley Hendrickson, Tommy Kedar, Mahsa Khodabakhsh, Allison Knowles, Kerry Lilley, Quinn Morgan, Stella Park, Brandon Pipkon, Antonio Plutino, Isabella Polenghi-Gross, Grace Liu, Erin Reese, Valerie Schneider, Richard Steckel, Bettie Steckel, Bob and Karla Treasure, Bette Yozell, and Lisa Zahner.

I'm so grateful to my early reviewers for your feedback, insight, and guidance: Beth Gillespie, Evelyne Lambrecht, Jennifer Meredith, Jacqueline Miller, and Heather Morgan.

Thank you to my editor Katie Chambers and my proof-reader Leona Skene.

And a very special thank you to Roberto Giannicola. I love every chapter with you.

ABOUT THE AUTHOR

Robin Treasure is a multilingual world traveler who has lived abroad in several different countries (Italy, UAE, and Costa Rica). After a successful first career in Rome and San Francisco as an Italian translator, she transitioned into sales with the key transferable skill needed in any capacity, in any language: emotionally intelligent communication.

When she is not writing a book, speaking, coaching, or learning a new language, you can find Robin hiking, taking a barre class, or spending time with her daughter and loved ones.

To learn more about Robin and her services visit: robin-treasure.com

THANK YOU FOR READING

HEART-POWERED SALES!

I have two requests:

1. Please leave an honest review on Amazon.
2. Think of a friend or colleague who would benefit from this book and share your copy or recommend it to them.

Feel free to email comments, feedback, or questions to robin@robintreasure.com

With love and gratitude,
Robin

Made in United States
Orlando, FL
02 February 2022

14332867R00148